Cambridge E

Elements in Leadership
edited by
Ronald Riggio
Claremont McKenna College
Susan Murphy
University of Edinburgh
Georgia Sorenson
University of Cambridge

CULTURAL DYNAMICS AND LEADERSHIP

An Interpretive Approach

Nathan W. Harter
Christopher Newport University

CAMBRIDGE
UNIVERSITY PRESS

CAMBRIDGE
UNIVERSITY PRESS

University Printing House, Cambridge CB2 8BS, United Kingdom

One Liberty Plaza, 20th Floor, New York, NY 10006, USA

477 Williamstown Road, Port Melbourne, VIC 3207, Australia

314–321, 3rd Floor, Plot 3, Splendor Forum, Jasola District Centre,
New Delhi – 110025, India

103 Penang Road, #05–06/07, Visioncrest Commercial, Singapore 238467

Cambridge University Press is part of the University of Cambridge.

It furthers the University's mission by disseminating knowledge in the pursuit of
education, learning, and research at the highest international levels of excellence.

www.cambridge.org
Information on this title: www.cambridge.org/9781009009874
DOI: 10.1017/9781009002066

© Nathan W. Harter 2022

First published 2022

A catalogue record for this publication is available from the British Library.

ISBN 978-1-009-00987-4 Paperback
ISSN 2631-7796 (online)
ISSN 2631-7788 (print)

Cultural Dynamics and Leadership

An Interpretive Approach

Elements in Leadership

DOI: 10.1017/9781009002066
First published online: March 2022

Nathan W. Harter
Christopher Newport University

Author for correspondence: Nathan W. Harter, nathan.harter@cnu.edu

Abstract: The intersection of leadership and culture is undertheorized. This Element looks behind familiar titles in leadership at materials from anthropology, sociology, and history to gain a more nuanced understanding of culture. Of particular relevance is an interpretive approach, elaborated in the works of Simmel, Cassirer, Ortega y Gasset, and Gadamer. A five-part schema examines permutations pertaining to the relationship between culture and leadership – as separate, conflicting, derivative, or engaged – with the most attractive being the possibility that leadership and culture are mutually constituting. To explain cultural change, Ortega y Gasset suggested as a unit of analysis the idea of a generation, illustrated in a historical account of translating the Bible. Archer proposed as a mechanism for cultural change the idea of social morphogenesis, which this Element applies to evolving issues of race in the civic order. This process is illustrated in the thinking of pundit William F. Buckley, Jr.

Keywords: Leadership, culture, hermeneutics, social morphogenesis, William F. Buckley Jr.

ISBNs: 9781009009874 (PB), 9781009002066 (OC)
ISSNs: 2631-7796 (online), 2631-7788 (print)

Contents

1 What Is Culture?

The term "culture" has been difficult to define because it pertains to an array of different types of things: mental, normative, behavioral, functional, historical, and symbolic. For this reason, an alternative approach would be to identify various dimensions. This section identifies a number of these dimensions: between culture in the abstract and concrete cultures; between a culture as a whole and its parts; between two coexisting cultures; between that which persists and that which changes; between the collective and the individual; between what lies in front of consciousness and what lies behind; between culture as an interior phenomenon and culture as an exterior phenomenon; and between descriptive and normative claims. Despite the experience of culture as a coherent whole, no culture is a monolith. Instead, each culture is subject to elaborations, accretions, syncretisms, and reinterpretations.

1.1 Introduction

Leadership always takes place within a context. Scholars have accounted for the importance of the context for more than a hundred years (see e.g. Bryman, Stephens, & Campo, 1996; Fiedler, 1972, citing Terman, 1904; McCusker, Foti, & Abraham, 2019, pp. 10–18; Osborn, Hunt, & Jauch, 2002; Wren & Swatez, 1995). Context is also known as the environment, situation, circumstances, or setting for such things as leadership. As political scientist Archie Brown (2014) wrote, "Leadership is highly contextual and what is appropriate or possible in one situation may be inappropriate or unattainable in another" (p. 25).[1]

That context includes culture. A thorough understanding of leadership therefore requires an understanding of the relationship between leadership and culture. A study of leadership without factoring culture is inherently limited (Colvin, 1996, p. 42, citing Sergiovanni, 1992). What follows is intended for students of leadership, so that they might account successfully for the relevant culture. The salient nexus between leadership and culture will be seen to be the topic of *shared values*.

This Element exists for students of leadership to examine that relationship. But it will not be easy. For one thing, experts have never settled on definitions for either term. Students of leadership already know about these struggles (e.g. Rost, 1993). In a similar fashion, students of culture frequently complain that the term "culture" is vague, fuzzy, even broad to the point of being useless (e.g. Alvesson, 1993; Archer, 1996; Eagleton, 2000). That possibility should not

---

[1] Robert Colvin (1996) cited Lewin (1951) for the proposition that B = F (P, E), where Behavior (B) is a Function (F) of Person (P) and Environment (E) (p. 33).

deter scholars and practitioners, however, inasmuch as something called culture plainly influences leadership. What then can we say that culture is? Here is where we shall begin.

1.2 Attempts at a Theoretical Definition for the Term "Culture"

Aristotle taught that after affirming that something exists, such as culture, the next logical question pertains to its definition (McKeon, 1947, *Posterior Analytics* 2.1). An answer to that question usually requires considerable analysis. Often, readers are satisfied initially with a *stipulative definition*, as a way of accessing what the writer is trying to say – "By X, I shall mean Y." Nevertheless, one should not want to accept anybody's bare stipulation and leave it at that. As students of leadership, we are more interested in what is known as a *theoretical definition* (see Copi, 1978, pp. 135–141).

The term "culture" appears in many academic disciplines already. To begin, one might start by consulting the standard reference works, such as an encyclopedia or dictionary. *The Cambridge Advanced Learner's Dictionary and Thesaurus* (2021) for example refers to:

> the way of life, especially the general customs and beliefs, of a particular group of people at a particular time [and more particularly in the social sciences to] the way of life of a particular people, esp. as shown in their ordinary behavior and habits, their attitudes toward each other, and their moral and religious beliefs.

One could trace the etymology of the word to find its origins or roots pertaining to the attentive care to one's farmland, as in cultivation of a field, or one's worship, as suggested by the term "cult." By gathering such materials, one acquires a *lexical definition* – that is, how the term is commonly used. In our case, though, we would be especially interested in the usage among experts in our field of study (Gardner with Laskin, 1995). Presumably, they would have been working toward that elusive theoretical definition.

Toward that end, we would be advised to begin with an understanding of the pioneering literature. In leadership studies, that would begin back in 1980, when Geert Hofstede published *Culture's Consequences*. In 1985, Edgar Schein wrote the first edition of *Organizational Culture and Leadership*. Not long after, in 1991, Robert House conceived the worldwide study of leadership under different cultures, adopting the acronym for Global Leadership and Organizational Behavior Effectiveness (GLOBE), a project that launched a multitude of publications by many authors, such that House alone does not get all of the credit. Nevertheless, these authors in particular (Hofstede, Schein, and House) influence all subsequent work regarding the topic of leadership and culture. Then, in

1994, Gilbert Fairholm published *Leadership and the Culture of Trust*. More recently, Mats Alvesson used a Critical Theory approach. These are all formative influences on the field of leadership studies.

Needless to say, these formative influences do not always agree with one another. Furthermore, some of them focus more on organizational culture, whereas others focus on what we might call national or societal culture. Delving into this literature, one finds empirical research, advice, and critical perspectives. Yet, these voices were anticipated years beforehand in fields such as philosophy, sociology, and anthropology – parent disciplines out of which leadership studies has emerged. For the sake of thoroughness, therefore, perhaps we need to consult these seminal sources first, works that can be said to lay behind leadership studies. Let us briefly undertake an archaeology of the term – a strategy that will omit many works in the literature of leadership studies that presume to address the topic.

Academic attempts to define culture begin with Edward Burnett Tylor's tentative effort from 1871, when he suggested that culture can be defined as "that complex whole which includes knowledge, belief, art, morals, law, custom, and any other capabilities and habits acquired by man as a member of society" (p. 1). A couple of pages later, he referred to "the condition of knowledge, religion, art, custom, and the like" (p. 5). From this perspective, culture is seen to be a collection or array – not only a collection of many things, but of many different *kinds* of things.

In 1952, Alfred L. Kroeber and Clyde Kluckhohn (1963) published a critical review of subsequent definitions, giving pride of place to Tylor, of course, but then tracing a development in the literature of the social sciences – and most importantly, of anthropology. They catalogued attempts to define the term, grouping them into types and demonstrating not only the variety (a conceptual array) but also the history (a chronological array). Rather than close around a consensus choice, they found that the definitions just keep proliferating (Kroeber & Kluckhohn, 1963; see Goldstein, 1957, pp. 1075–1077).

In light of a plurality of definitions, Meagan Clough (2002) has proposed a taxonomy of types of definitions (p. 102; see also Hecht, Baldwin, & Faulkner, 2006, p. 54; Kroeber & Kluckhohn, 1963, p. 318; Schein, 2004, p. 12f), pointing out that some definitions emphasize:

- what individual members think, believe, or feel, consciously or unconsciously (*mental/ideological*);
- what members think that they ought to do or value (*normative*);
- what members and groups actually do (*behavioral/customary*);
- how members and groups cope (*functional*);

- what previous members did (*historical/lore*); and
- what things are supposed to mean (*symbolic*, including language and the arts).

To be thorough, anything we mean by the term "culture" should probably be regarded as an integration of all of these, which frankly leaves us with a vast, unwieldy content.

In 2006, John Baldwin, Sandra Faulkner, Michael Hecht, and Sheryl Lindsley edited an update on the Kroeber and Kluckhohn critical review. After validating some of what had been established back in 1952, they challenge other aspects. Even so, no matter how you define the term, say Baldwin, Faulkner and Hecht, you run the risk of omitting or overlooking some aspect that seems to fall outside the frame of what you were trying to study (2006, p. 17). It would be easy (or at least understandable) in certain contexts to miss what they call the interstices and the marginal. That is to say that even in the presence of multiple, inconsistent definitions in the academic literature, there will be aspects of culture that go unaccounted for.

Given the complex, limited, and evolving array of possible definitions, perhaps "culture" is what philosophers call an "essentially contested concept" (Gallie, 1956; see Rosaldo, 2006, p. x), forever out of reach. Maybe it was not meant to be defined once-and-for-all. One writer suggested that culture has no essence (Cassirer, 1942/2000, p. 72).

Here then is one strategy for moving forward. Perhaps it helps to say what culture is not. For instance, culture is not the same thing as nature. If anything, it exists in contraposition to the natural world (Niebuhr, 1951, p. 32; cf. Ortega y Gasset, 1933/1961, pp. 41–45). As such, it is distinctly human – achieved by humans for the benefit of humans (Brunner, 1949, p. 127; Niebuhr, 1951, p. 33; see generally Baldwin, Faulkner, & Hecht, 2006; Fairholm, 1994, p. 39; Kroeber & Kluckhohn, 1963, pp. 37 & 165; Moody-Adams, 1997, p. 227 n. 7). We might say that nature in the form of life shapes man so that he participates in culture, which in turn shapes both him and nature (Ortega y Gasset, 1957, p. 31; cf. Geertz, 1973, pp. 46–49). Culture mediates between the individual human being and the natural world as a kind of second reality (Hofstede, Hofstede, & Minkov, 2010, p. 6; Ortega y Gasset, 1957, p. 175). It has even become so enveloping that most folks today consider their culture to be natural and think no more about it (Hofstede, Hofstede, & Minkov, 2010, p. 11; Ortega y Gasset, 1932, p. 65). Consequently, since it is not (like nature) passed down genetically, culture must be transmitted from one generation to the next in some other fashion, such as education (Brunner, 1949, p. 135; Clough, 2002, p. 87 f.; see Hofstede, Hofstede, & Minkov, 2010, p. 4 f.).

Culture is not the same as nature. Neither is culture individual, since nobody can claim his or her own idiosyncratic culture (Baldwin, Faulkner, & Hecht, 2006, p. 48, citing Seymour-Smith, 1986; see also Moody-Adams, 1997, pp. 19 f & 46). That is to say that we suppose culture to be social (Geertz, 1973, pp. 76 f. & 83; Hofstede, Hofstede, & Minkov, 2010, p. 6; Niebuhr, 1951, p. 32 f.). Nevertheless, it is only part of that which is social. Margaret Archer has consistently differentiated culture from social structures, such as religion and the state. In fact, she called it the *Fallacy of Conflation* to regard them all as the same thing (1996, p. xv; see Geertz, 1973, pp. 331 & 337). They are not. Culture is not the same thing as the social structures. The problem is that saying what culture is not, however, is inadvisable in a definition (Copi, 1978, p. 157 f.).

If we cannot get to what the term means by saying what it is not, here is a second strategy. Because the term is so broad and vague, we are often reduced to describing culture by means of simile and metaphor (Alvesson, 2002, ch. 2). Culture is all around us, for example, and yet inside of us. It is – like water to a fish – a habitation that we do not always even notice. William Donaldson refers to culture as a force field, an emergent property of social systems (2017, p. 100). Hofstede, Hofstede, and Minkov (2010) resort to the imagery of surface and depth (p. 7). Examples of metaphor can be multiplied. The problem is that a definition must not be so expressed (Copi, 1978, p. 156 f.). By this point, we seem no closer to our goal. Fortunately, there is another approach, a third strategy that deserves a closer look.

1.3 Dimensions to Culture

A different tactic for orienting oneself in unfamiliar territory is to use a number of dimensions based on available dichotomies, like consulting the cardinal compass points (see Baldwin, Faulkner, & Hecht, 2006, p. 24; Geertz, 1973, p. 354; Kroeber & Kluckhohn, 1963, p. 331). The following portion of this Section looks at the following seven dichotomies:

- *concrete* cultures that one experiences versus culture in the *abstract* that one conceptualizes;
- culture as a *whole* versus subcultures as *parts* of the whole;
- that which *changes* versus that which *persists*;
- *collective* level versus *individual* level;
- *conscious* elements versus *nonconscious* elements;
- understood from the *exterior* versus understood from the *interior*; and
- *descriptive* versus *prescriptive*.

1.3.1 Concrete versus Abstract

Part of the problem with defining a term such as "culture" is that nobody experiences culture in the abstract; we always experience a particular culture (Eagleton, 2000, p. 13; Niebuhr, 1951, p. 31). Pointing at concrete examples of culture as a way of defining the term *ostensively* will not work in this case. Pointing toward what exactly? If I ask, "What does the word mean?" – one cannot simply offer examples and expect me to understand.

In actual practice, culture itself is an *abstraction* from the *concrete* cultures one might attribute to different communities, such as different national cultures or organizational cultures. H. Richard Niebuhr stated it succinctly that "culture as we are concerned with it is not a particular phenomenon but the general one, though the general thing appears only in particular forms" (1951, p. 31). We can speak of Culture itself as a social fact, as a "general" thing, even though in actual experience it would be more accurate to speak in terms of cultures in the plural. An individual human being experiences discrete cultures (*living* in a culture, *observing* a culture, *pledging allegiance to* a culture) and also, from one step removed, ascribes to them as a class the single label of Culture (see Kroeber & Kluckhohn, 1963, p. 367). You can treat culture as something concrete, to be *experienced*, as well as an abstraction, to be *conceived*, just as you can speak in terms of individual leaders (as concrete exemplars) and the phenomenon of leadership (as an abstract process). Donald Fiske put it plainly when he wrote that "all levels above the bottom one are abstractions" (1986, p. 64). To this extent, culture (as we shall intend the term) is both concrete and abstract.

1.3.2 Whole versus Parts of the Whole

Even within concrete cultures, there will be subcultures – some of which emerge in opposition to or as an alternative to the dominant culture, while others simply cluster around particular lifestyles, such as thug life, biker gangs, religious sects, and ethnic enclaves (see e.g. Schouten & McAlexander, 1995). One can speak of the culture of a religion, the culture within a socioeconomic status, the culture of a geographical region, the culture in an organization or an occupation, and so forth (Cohen, 2009, p. 195; Hofstede, 1993/1995, p. 269; Kroeber & Kluckhohn, 1963, p. 309; Schein, 2004, p. 20 f.). One can even describe a hierarchy of "nesting" cultures, one within the other (see Kroeber & Kluckhohn, 1963, p. 367). Here, we encounter a contrast of some importance – in this instance, a contrast between a culture of the *whole* and a culture of the *part*. And there remains a multitude of ways of subdividing that whole, like slicing a watermelon from any one of several angles.

Of particular interest to students of leadership is the emergence of counter-cultures, challenging the status quo (see generally, Roberts, 1978). In the Soviet Union, for instance, the authorities were not sure how to manage the folk traditions of comedy, carnival, and satire, because these were perceived to be countercultural and contrary to good order, inversions of authority devoted to mocking the powers-that-be, despite the fact that what was actually new to the people was the insertion of Soviet values (Lachmann, Eshelman, & Davis, 1988).

1.3.3 Change versus Persistence

Culture is not a static thing. Every concrete culture changes over time, so that one is always dealing with a moving target (Baldwin, Faulkner, & Hecht, 2006, p. 17). The study of this phenomenon has been named "cultural dynamics" (Hatch, 1993). For instance, the United States of the 1920s (with the golden age of jazz, flappers, and Prohibition) is noticeably different from the United States of the 1960s (with Woodstock, the Vietnam War, and NASA's Apollo project). Nevertheless, culture persists over time as well, exhibiting a history (Tylor, 1871, p. 7; see generally Kroeber & Kluckhohn, 1963, p. 312), inasmuch as one of the central features of culture is that it must be "transmitted" from one generation to the next (Cohen, 2009, p. 195; see Kroeber & Kluckhohn, 1963, p. 164 f.). Edgar Schein said of culture that it is deep and stable (2004, p. 14). Yet, it is also true that one can observe elements of culture changing (Tylor, 1871, p. 15), as for example the evolution of personal computing in the twenty-first century. Certain features "survive," while other features from the past might "revive" (Tylor, 1871, p. 17). An integral part of developing any science of culture would be trying to understand these processes – that is, the antecedents and the consequences across time (see Durkheim, 1895/1938, p. 143). What in fact *changes*, and what *persists*?

The Spaniard José Ortega y Gasset noted the inherent tension between stability, on the one hand, and vitality, on the other. He wrote that "uncultured life is barbarism, devitalized culture is byzantinism" (1933/1961, p. 46). Part of what it means to be cultured is to discern the difference between durable innovations, on the one hand, and fashions and fads, on the other (Ortega y Gasset, 1932, p. 116; see de Tarde, 1895/1903).

1.3.4 Collective versus Individual Level

Not everyone walks around with an equal share in the dominant culture. Some are connoisseurs of wine or scrimshaw or ballet. Others we might characterize as lowbrow or uncultured, as though there would be degrees of enculturation.

We speak in ordinary usage of cultivating one's judgment or taste, which is a way of talking about learning how to appreciate the finer things in life. Lévi-Strauss called this "enlightened enrichment" (1988/1991, p. 164). Nevertheless, one can detect patterns throughout a body of people and across time. Thus, a culture has to be sufficiently widespread to serve as a kind of generalization, as something shared (Tylor, 1871, p. 10 f.). Culture belongs to that which is "extra-organic" or "super-organic" (Kroeber & Kluckhohn, 1963, p. 13). In the study of culture, one must reconcile what one observes at the level of the *collective* (or macro) with what happens at the *individual* (or micro) level. In other words, these are two methods of inquiry for the same phenomenon, from above (so to speak) and from below (Tylor, 1871, p. 13).

1.3.5 Conscious versus Nonconscious Elements

What follows is yet another distinction. Participants are often quite aware of specific elements of culture, such as festivals and exhibitions. They take great pride in them or devote resources to promoting them. They make jokes, let us say, or create classroom lessons out of these elements or circle holidays in red on their calendar. An entire nation can shut down for a few hours in order to follow the fortunes of its football team. Yet, at the same time, participants are not always conscious of other elements; these elements, such as language, are often taken for granted or assimilated so completely as to be transparent (Lévi-Strauss, 1988/1991, p. 39; see generally Polanyi, 2009). Kroeber and Kluckhohn (1963) insisted that the "analysis of a culture must encompass both the explicit and the implicit" (p. 121). The implicit, they wrote, "consists in those cultural themes of which there is characteristically no sustained and systematic awareness on the part of most members of a group" (p. 335). One might say that parts of culture are in front of the threshold of consciousness, whereas other parts lie behind.

1.3.6 Exterior versus Interior

One of the disciplines to investigate culture is psychology – and more specific-ally something known as cultural psychology (Cohen, 2009). Here, the focus is not exclusively on "what is inside the mind of people" (as one might suppose of a psychological approach) but also the social world (Cohen, 2009, p. 195 n. 1). We might say that there is an *interior* aspect of culture and an *exterior* aspect of culture (see generally Wilber, 1998). My tendency to identify with and conform to what I understand to be "my people" or "my community" is something different from the artifacts and practices that are out there, existing over against any lone individual social actor. I carry with me an identity that reflects who

I think that I am (e.g. many Lutherans offer a prayer of thanksgiving over meals); also, however, there exist paintings and statues and architecture and laws and markets and the very language in which I participate, even though I never created any of them or chose them. They are there, as part of my environment, surrounding me. The way that Kroeber and Kluckhohn (1963) put it, both the inward and the outward would be relevant to any study of culture, so long as one does not confuse the two (p. 222 f; Baldwin, Faulkner, & Hecht, 2006, p. 11).

What we are calling the "outward" has been subdivided conceptually between the objective culture of artifacts and activities that can be sensed, on the one hand, and the subjective culture of thoughts, beliefs, and values that must be felt or thought (Baldwin, Faulkner, & Hecht, 2006, p. 12). This second or subjective culture is different from the "inward" in that the subjective is still out there in the group or society, existing not in the mind or imagination of the individual human being, but instead in his or her environment, often preexisting the individual human being and serving as an ideal or imperative.

One example of subjective culture that might not be shared inwardly is patriotism; the positive meaning attached to an anthem or a flag is not universal. It must be taught, if only vicariously, and there will almost always be members of the group who reject patriotism (or the excesses of patriotism, or the implications of patriotism). One must keep these two separate, especially in leadership studies, where so much of what a leader does occurs at the tangent: What is subjective is sometimes exterior to the individual social actor (Searle, 2006).

1.3.7 Descriptive versus Prescriptive

As for another important dichotomy, making these distinctions in a *descriptive* fashion between one side and another is not the same thing as passing judgment on whether one culture (or one cultural practice or artifact) is somehow better than another. That kind of evaluative or *prescriptive* comparison of better and worse is a separate undertaking ... and for scientists often objectionable.

Anyone can pile up reasons why coming to a definition of such a term as "culture" with so many distinctions and dichotomies would be difficult. We have found boundaries between culture in the abstract and concrete cultures; between a culture as a whole and its part; between two coexisting cultures; between that which persists and that which changes; between the collective and the individual; between what lies in front of consciousness and what lies behind; between culture as an interior phenomenon and culture as an exterior phenomenon; between descriptive and normative claims. In fairness, the boundaries between these various sides of each dichotomy are rarely hard and fast. We can use these dichotomies for our conceptual purposes, even though in actual experience they often bleed into one another (see Lévi-Strauss, 1988/1991, p. 152).

1.4 On the Purported Coherence of a Culture

Whereas culture is indeed an array of different kinds of things, nonetheless it possesses a relatively coherent structure such that we can refer to it loosely as one thing – it is both a totality and an enumeration (Kroeber & Kluckhohn, 1963, pp. 85, 120, 169, & 311; see also Faulkner et al., 2006, pp. 31–37). Ruth Benedict, writing in 1934, explained in some detail that culture can be said to constellate, integrating so many disparate elements into a more-or-less coherent whole, which she called its "configuration" (1934/2005, pp. 22, 37 f, 45–56, & 223–229; see Alvesson, 1993, p. 75; Cassirer, 1942/2000, p. 123; Geertz, 1973, p. 17). Kroeber and Kluckhohn wrote:

> Every culture is a structure – not just a haphazard collection of all the different physically possible and functionally effective patterns of belief and action but an interdependent *system* with its forms segregated and arranged in a manner which is *felt* as appropriate. (1963, p. 337 f.)

Ortega y Gasset adopted the metaphor of clothing that should fit the body so that nothing chafes. Given the contours of the body and its usual range of motion, you hardly notice what you are wearing (1940/1946, pp. 11–47). Culture is a lot like that. One might call it a suitable *ensemble*. Briefly, then, according to a static model, culture can be imagined as a field with some degree of order.

Whatever we might mean by the term, Margaret Archer (1996) insisted that culture is no monolith; it is not one broad, undifferentiated web or seamless garment (see generally ch. 1; also pp. xvii & 27). Instead, upon closer inspection, it is rife with conflict, inconsistencies, and underdeveloped aspects. Empirically, there is more than one culture in the world, and they are not identical. More importantly, within a given culture, she distinguished (a) the *cultural system* as an entity or thing from (b) the *sociocultural interactions* that constitute daily life. These do not work in lockstep, even if they are interdependent – that is, they are not tightly integrated with one another. Even within each category (cultural system and sociocultural interactions, respectively), they are still not wholly integrated either. Otherwise, there would be no potential for change. Anthropologists and sociologists operated for some time on the assumption that all of this was fully integrated and constituted a complete whole, as though comprised of "strong and coherent patterning" (1996, p. 2).

A particular tribe was presumed to possess a single, unitary culture. Archer utterly destroys the myth of cultural integration (1996, ch. 1).

To the outside observer, a culture is neither logically consistent nor causally coherent, even when it feels that way to participants (Archer, 1996, p. 4; see Geertz, 1973, p. 406 f; Moody-Adams, 1997, pp. 9, 44, 49, & 63). Archer sees no reason to accept the participants' version at face value. Besides, even if it was fully integrated, which she denies, one would be justified in asking: What about the occasions that challenge a prevailing culture – occasions such as deviance from within, invasion from without, and residual taboos that nobody wants to talk about publicly? Any community open to the outside world (e.g. by means of trade and exogamy) constantly runs the risk of heteronomy. This can be seen most vividly in port cities, where the culture is already more tolerant of aberration (see e.g. de Landa, 2000). But then, at all times, even the strictest regime must figure out how to accommodate the "vertical invasion of barbarism," known as childbirth.[2] No, says Archer, far better to presuppose pluralism, incursions, and periods of transition (Archer, 1996, p. 9). What she was suggesting is yet another polarity to be taken seriously, which is the polarity between a culture's coherence and its incoherence, to the extent this is made manifest in a culture that is "tight" or "loose" (Gelfand, 2019).

Perhaps culture is better understood as a vital process, a pulsating drama, with its cast of characters, including the teacher, the traitor, the heretic, the artist, the visionary, and the ambitious. Fissures in culture make these characters come to life, giving them an excuse to play their various parts. In the ensuing drama, these conflicts and inconsistencies in the culture will be revealed, exploited, exacerbated, and possibly resolved. Furthermore, Archer accepted the possibility in social life of absurdity and ambivalence (1996, p. 11; see Merton, 1976). Also, there is evidence that in many societies, the culture fails to account for what she calls "loose ends" – pieces that don't fit, oddities, quirks, and gaps (1996, p. 15). Moody-Adams called them "internal outsiders" (1997, p. 68). Consequently, the community may try to ignore these possibilities or banish outright the members who represent such loose ends, thereby retaining and projecting the illusion of coherence. One saw this recently when a political leader in Iran was mistranslated to declare that of course they had no homosexuals (Reuters, 2007); obviously, they do; at the time of this writing, Iran's legal system acknowledges this implicitly by condemning them to death.

Even in the simplest tribe, where the range of life's possibilities are limited and members devote their waking hours to subsistence, there is no reason to

---

[2] Cultural transmission from one generation to the next is likewise incomplete, irregular, and makeshift (Faulkner et al., 2006, p. 51).

assume that their lack of alternatives denotes cultural uniformity. That the culture in the tribe is fully integrated is an optical illusion (Archer, 1996, p. 12; see Schein, 2004, pp. 30–36) – an illusion mostly to its participant, so that if he or she is your source of ethnology, you may be consulting an unreliable informant. But even if you did presuppose full integration for these aboriginal peoples, wrote Archer, then how do you explain the historical fact that the vast and bewildering cultures in the twenty-first century ever evolved from such a tight and unyielding beginning (see Hofstede, Hofstede, & Minkov, 2010, pp. 453–455)? Archer detected in cultures a series of transitions as elaborations, accretions, syncretisms, and reinterpretations (1996, p. 18 f.).[3] We have to allow for cultural dynamics. And cultural dynamics derive from and create these fissures. So, it is in the interest of leadership studies to accept Archer's position about the myth of cultural integration. Otherwise, leadership does not seem to make much sense.

None of which is to say that there are no patterns and continuities in culture. One can find degrees of congruence in any sustainable culture. Part of the study of leadership in culture is to detect these patterns. There is no need to go to the other extreme and infer randomness. Archer was simply cautioning against presuppositions familiar to anthropology and sociology that do not fit the reality that makes our research so interesting and frankly necessary. In fact, by adopting Archer's position, the patterns that are found to emerge would be that much more remarkable.

A further indicator that culture is no monolith arises in the popular "iceberg" imagery, where the outward or overt expressions of culture, such as artifacts and ceremonies, suggest a deeper layer of meaning (e.g. Hofstede, Hofstede, & Minkov, 2010, p. 6; Schein, 2004, ch. 2). We can think of there being layers to culture from symbols (at the surface), to heroes, rituals, and finally (at its depth) to values. Culture cannot be understood separated from a consideration of certain values that imply collective purpose (Colvin, 1996, p. 84; see generally Niebuhr, 1951, pp. 29–39). Kroeber and Kluckhohn explained that "values provide the only basis for the fully intelligible comprehension of culture, because the actual organization of all cultures is primarily in terms of their values" (1963, p. 340).

That deeper layer that Hofstede had placed at the center of the culture would be the hardest part for leadership to alter (Hofstede, Hofstede, & Minkov, 2010, p. 19; see Fairholm, 1994, p. 49; Schein, 2004, p. 31). There may be espoused values (which would be conscious) or underlying assumptions (which would be

---

[3] The metaphor used by Geertz is that at any given point in time, a culture is bending backward toward its tradition and also leaning forward at the same time (1973, p. 320).

nonconscious). In some instances, espoused values clash with underlying assumptions, leading to accusations of hypocrisy (Schein, 2004, p. 30). Furthermore, pluralism holds that these underlying values (even if they are genuine) are not always compatible one with another (Bernstein, 1997). Some philosophers such as Isaiah Berlin see no reason to assume that one's value structure is unified and coherent (e.g. Jahanbegloo, 1995). In many cases, those values are logically incompatible with each other, yet they are held together somehow in what Niebuhr called "tolerable conflict" (1951, p. 38; see Alvesson, 1993, pp. 63 & 111; Benedict, 1934/2005, p. 228; Schein, 2004, p. 17). So that even here, at the core, when one talks about "values," culture can be seen to be capable of profound and intractable contradictions. Such is the abiding dissonance in every culture. Leadership exists in part to address that abiding dissonance (Colvin, 1996, p. 88 f.) – whether to reconcile or exacerbate, entrench or overthrow. Likely, there will be leadership on both sides of the barricades.

1.5 Concluding Thoughts

The search for a theoretical definition has brought us through a variety of previous attempts without arriving at much that is definitive. We can say with some confidence that culture is a dynamic array of types of things in response to nature that give meaning to a group of people across time. We can study its various dimensions without (a) reducing culture to either one of two poles and without (b) presupposing that any culture is altogether static or monolithic.

2 An Interpretive Approach to Culture

The study of culture originates in a fundamental split between the mathematical-physical sciences, on the one side, and the sociohistorical, on the other. The latter requires a different kind of knowledge (*verstehen*), using different methods because of a different subject matter. According to an interpretative approach known as the Postulate of Subjective Meaning, students engage in double-loop hermeneutics in order to discern the underlying intention of human behavior. In order to remember and communicate experiences, people adopt symbols such as language to represent what they are trying to say. Culture provides a wealth of these symbolic forms through which participants express their thoughts and ideas, although as it happens, these symbols often constrain one another's understanding and likewise change across time. One strategy for interpreting symbols is to track down the originating question to which they are a response, for it is the *question* that sets into motion the dynamics that we attribute to leadership.

2.1 Introduction

Multiple disciplines address the topic of culture, a fact that indicates the breadth of the topic and also exemplifies why the study of culture can be so confusing. There is no single literature to consult. Scholars can all cite different authorities, who rely on completely different models and vocabularies. The term "culture" is itself a versatile symbol for many things. One may wonder what a science of culture might look like when you have scholars dedicated to cultural sociology, cultural psychology, cultural politics, cultural history, cultural management, biocultural anthropology, cultural chemistry, cultural technology, intercultural communication, ethnic studies, ethnolinguistics, ethnomathematics, media studies, and culture in cognitive science, let alone the arts and humanities.

The following section offers a brief history and explanation of one approach – an interpretive approach in Western academe. Then, it relies primarily on the work of Georg Simmel and his student Ernst Cassirer by addressing how human beings make sense of personal experience in their usage of symbols. In this way, we might begin to understand the construction of a culture comprised of elaborate constellations of symbols and images with their accompanying meanings. After this, since leadership depends on consensus – that is, on an interpersonal dimension – the section begins to address how human beings make sense of one another's usage of symbols and images. Obviously, a complete description of what is known about this social process exceeds the scope of one element, yet even here one can recognize an opportunity for leaders and their followers to penetrate the symbols and images in which they traffic by imagining the question that prompted them in the first place. As Hans-Georg Gadamer pointed out, the process known as *hermeneutics* generates fresh meanings that would never have occurred to participants in isolation. Often, creative interpretation of existing symbols is precisely what leadership elicits.

2.2 The Emergence of the "Interpretive" Approach

Leadership studies flows primarily out of the sociohistorical sciences. These sciences can boast a long history. In the German tradition, Martin Luther (1483–1546) insisted on the dual nature of humanity: for him, the human being is both physical (and therefore a bodily object) and spiritual.[4] A complete understanding of what it means to be human, therefore, would include both aspects; yet

---

[4] The distinction did not originate with Luther. It can be found in the letters of Paul the Apostle, for example, and then again in the anthropology of Augustine, just to cite a couple of prominent Christian sources. Isaiah Berlin credits Giambattista Vico with the distinction (1969/1979, pp. 111–119). Barry Cooper also credits Aristotle regarding *physis* and *nomos* (2020, p. 25). Yet, Luther can be identified as the proximate cause for what took place in German universities over the next couple of centuries.

they are complementary aspects of the one reality, requiring different ways of knowing.[5] Immanuel Kant (1724–1804) formalized this distinction, saying that as part of one reality, there are two worlds – that is, the world of phenomena and the world of noumena. The latter stood for an irreducibly conscious and self-determining subject, the locus of free will, which is the ground of all ethics (see generally Cooper, 2020, pp. 22–26; Levine, 1995, ch. 9). This conceptual split in Luther and then in Kant would harden over time.

In 1810, the reformation of the Prussian university system under Wilhelm von Humboldt regrouped the academic disciplines on a large scale (see Gebhardt & Cooper, 1995, p. xi), preserving Kant's (and Luther's) distinction that there are two ways of knowing what it means to be human. By the time of the unification of Germany in 1871, the disciplines were struggling to establish their discrete foundations. The mathematical-physical sciences such as physics, chemistry, and biology were enjoying such undeniable success that many across academe were calling for the other disciplines to mimic their methods – imitation being the sincerest form of flattery. This call to render all science as analogous to the mathematical-physical sciences is known as positivism, and it still exists today in one form or another (see generally Kolakowski, 1966/1972). One might think of positivism as an attempt to collapse the old Luther/Kant distinction and subsume all science as strictly natural. Rudolf Carnap (1934/1995), to cite one example, tried to make the case that any understanding of reality not grounded in physics is literal nonsense.

In opposition to positivism, however, there arose three rival conceptions. These rivals sought to ground their disciplines in something *other than* the mathematical-physical sciences. Wilhelm Windelband and Heinrich Rickert emphasized the study of culture (*kultur*); Wilhelm Dilthey emphasized the study of spirit or mind (*Geist*); and (occupying a lesser status, yet foreshadowing leadership studies) *Staatswissenschaften* emphasized "the personification of power and rulership" in such disciplines as politics and law (Gebhardt & Cooper, 1995, p. xiv). Together, they tried to make the case for the following three things: different *methods* would be required in order to acquire a different *kind of knowledge* because of a difference in the *subject matter* (see generally Levine, 1995, ch. 9). For our purposes, we will refer to the two resulting alternatives as the mathematical-physical sciences, on the one hand, and the sociohistorical sciences, on the other.

Windelband, Rickert, Dilthey, and their allies would each concede that a scientist could certainly study human beings as objects by using the usual

---

[5] For Luther, humanity is not some combination of two different things that we now call spirit and flesh; a human being is a whole that can be regarded in two different ways (see Kantonen, 1972).

methods of the mathematical-physical sciences, which Anthony Giddens called *single-loop hermeneutics* (1993, p. 65). Physicians, for example, need this expertise in order to do their job. Nevertheless, that approach yields a different kind of knowledge. What the social scientists sought to do in various ways was to understand the *meanings* that people attach to their actions – *double-loop hermeneutics* (Giddens, 1993, p. 168). Over time, these pioneers in the sociohistorical sciences disagreed among themselves and their positions evolved, but versions of them survive to this day.

It is interesting to read the most eminent scholars trying to find their way forward through the divide. Some would still prefer to collapse the socio-historical into the mathematical-physical sciences, as with positivism, or collapse the mathematical-physical sciences into the sociohistorical. Others accept the two approaches as permanently juxtaposed in a stark dichotomy. Still others hope to integrate them into one overarching set of complementary methods (e.g. Giddens, 1984; Wilber, 1998).

Here is how one philosopher navigated the divide. During a survey of the sociohistorical sciences, Jürgen Habermas tried to make sense of this dichotomy as follows: "Social action belongs to the class of intentional actions, which we grasp by reconstructing their meaning. Social facts can be understood in terms of motivations" (1988, p. 11; see also Benedict, 1934/2005, p. 49). He went on to categorize social action as "behavior that is subjectively meaningful, that is, oriented to a subjectively intended meaning, and thus also motivated. It can be appropriately understood only with reference to the goals and values to which the acting subject is oriented" (1988, p. 53). Thus, "observable social action must be grasped from the perspective of the acting subject himself, a perspective that is removed from direct observation; that is, it must be 'understood'" (1988, p. 54). Habermas did make a concession: "In ethology, the study of animal behavior, objective methods have proved successful. Goal-directed, adaptive behavior can be grasped and analyzed without reference to intentions" (1988, p. 60). "Actions [on the other hand] cannot be understood without reference to the intentions that guide them; that is, independently of something like ideas, they cannot be studied at all" (1988, p. 71).

In another context, Donald Levine called this the Postulate of Subjective Meaning (1995, p. 187). Two people can do the same thing for entirely different reasons, just as two people can do two entirely different things for exactly the same reason. Often, there is no way to make sense of outward behavior until you understand what the other person may have been thinking. Clifford Geertz credits the philosopher Gilbert Ryle for making the distinction between a *thin description*, on the one hand, and a *thick description*, on the other (1973, ch. 1). A thin description simply describes, from the exterior, setting forth what is there to observe, such as an eyelid's contraction, whereas a thick description explores its meaning in the cultural context as a wink (see also Wilber, 1998). The apparent integration of any given culture overlooks the fact that despite some outward uniformity (according to one's thin description), the participants bring different, even sometimes incompatible interpretations of what it all means (Moody-Adams, 1997, pp. 49 & 147). More evidently, outsiders such as investigators into the dynamics of leadership must resort to their own interpretations about meanings, which is indeed possible inasmuch "no culture is a windowless monad" (Moody-Adams, 1997, p. 57).

How is that interpretation to be done? Dilthey had argued that "to understand the meaning of an actor's experience requires a special kind of cognition, which contrasts with that used in the sciences of natural phenomena" (Levine, 1995, p. 195). In other words, for anyone to make a science of those symbolic aspects of culture requires *Verstehen*, an approach that has been elaborated since in the practice of hermeneutics (cf. Giddens, 1993, p. 158).

In order to conduct these hermeneutics, we will consider the task of representing the meaning of personal experience in the form of symbols. After that, we will consider the task of interpreting the use of these symbols by other people. That is to say, I need symbols in order to understand the world; and I need symbols that you share with me in order for us to understand the world together.

2.3 Making Sense of One's Personal Experience by Means of Culture

Max Weber enjoys the greater reputation today among sociologists, yet he acknowledged that Simmel's analysis of a theory of *Verstehen* was more developed (Levine, 1995, p. 205, citing Weber in 1905). Horst Helle has written that Simmel (and not Weber) is regarded by sociologists as the founder of the interpretive school (2013, p. 19). Accordingly, this section begins with him and with one of his most celebrated students, Ernst Cassirer. Walker Percy remarked that "Cassirer's contribution has been described as the first philosophy of culture" (1954–1975, p. 222). What follows in this section depends predominately on their work.

As a practical matter, one begins life and leadership in a world of preexisting cultural forms, transmitted from prior generations, many of which are taken for granted. These forms include language, law, and the arts. Their purpose and meaning are not always clear. In many cases, they are not even conscious. Nevertheless, the lives of participants will tend to flow into these forms by default, like pouring melted wax into a mold. The survival of a cultural form indicates that it serves some present function, even though the landscape is also littered with forms that are merely vestigial, left over from a previous age, such as the ritual of when a father gives away his daughter as a bride.

The meaning of these preexisting cultural forms requires interpretation in a process known as *cultural hermeneutics* (Oakes, 1980, p. 58). "The science of culture teaches us to interpret symbols [and images] in order to decipher their hidden meaning – in order to make the life from which they originally emerged visible again" (Cassirer, 1942/2000, p. 86). Interpretation often relies on evidence of the state of mind of one's predecessor, but it is rarely that simple. For one thing, there might be no evidence whatsoever of what a predecessor intended, in which case one is left to make inferences (Simmel, 1916/2005; e.g. Hillman, 1986/2016, pp. 282–299). Often, the evidence that does survive requires further interpretation. The predecessor's own report, for example, such as a leader's memoir, might be incomplete, unclear, or insincere. Notice that we are assuming that the meaning was at one time consciously apprehended; on the contrary, we might be advised to consider the possibility that the unconscious contributes to the generation of symbols and images, making hermeneutic excavations even more problematic.[6] Furthermore, the cultural form to be interpreted originated within a context that also probably requires interpretation (Geertz, 1973, p. 9).[7] This is to say that the cultural form – whatever it is – was once a response to conditions that may no longer apply. Nevertheless, the form in question survives among us today. Leadership itself is such a form into which we pour our aspirations. We say, "Somebody ought to do something."

For the sake of thoroughness, the continuing existence of the form indicates that subsequent participants have found their own meaning in the cultural form – a meaning that might contradict the original (e.g. Pelikan, 1985). Needless to say, an interpretation can be mistaken. Alfred North Whitehead noted with chagrin that symbolism is fallible and that "the errors of mankind . . . spring from symbolism" (1927, p. 7). In addition, there is nothing to stop a participant from imbuing a cultural form with completely new meanings. A given symbol can have multiple meanings, even to the same person, and its meaning is also susceptible to change over time (Geertz, 1973, p. 212). A symbol can become an end in itself, separated entirely from any underlying meaning (Geertz, 1973, p. 335; Whitehead, 1927, p. 61).[8] In principle,

---

[6] The possibility of a role for the unconscious was developed primarily by Freudian and Jungian psychologists (see e.g. Freud, 2005; Jung, 1980; cf. MacIntyre, 1997). The philosopher Ludwig Wittgenstein advised against taking hermeneutics that far (1980, p. 23 e).

[7] For a context requiring its own interpretation, Michel Foucault adopted the term "épistème" (1966/1994).

[8] Leaders themselves frequently serve as symbols. Geertz remarked that once followers recognize that a leader is "just" a symbol, however, without any underlying meaning, that leader's authority tends to evaporate (1973, p. 212).

therefore, a cultural form can have an unlimited number of meanings in various stages of detail (Simmel, 1980, p. 114). Such is the empirical situation at the time leadership begins.

Originally, the cultural form emerged in response to someone's intent as an expression of their freedom (Simmel, 1918/1997, p. 23). Ernst Cassirer even asserted that the function of culture is to provide a venue in which participants get to experience and share their freedom (1942/2000, p. 97 ff.). As he put it abstractly, the spirit constantly exteriorizes itself (p. 107). Once brought into existence, however, a cultural form makes certain demands on its creators and their successors. Forms are capable of becoming self-perpetuating, influencing participants even after they no longer serve the original purpose (Helle, 2013, p. 3). Some forms such as oil painting are the product of generations of cultivation, consciously transmitted, where students are told, "This is how you do it." Other forms persist through a kind of inertia, like a neglected tennis court overgrown by weeds. Most significant for purposes of leadership is the fact that most forms originated at an earlier time in response to other, pre-existing forms, often as attempts to defy or escape the demands of these preexisting forms or otherwise to exert one's freedom of expression, even if all that they amount to are tweaks and adaptations, like varying the colors. The political office of the mayor was intended to replace the local lord or duke. The irony is that these expressions of freedom, such as new careers and personal relationships and institutions, once built, constrain freedom thereafter.[9] In response to which, each human being goes in search of his or her own liberation. Like an artist with a blank canvas and a loaded palette, the leader contemplates where to begin. Leadership begins by rejecting some existing alternative.[10]

Over time, culture becomes populated by a bewildering variety of forms that come into and also pass out of existence, persisting, changing, spreading, and presenting themselves to subsequent generations as opportunities, albeit coupled with corresponding imperatives.[11] You can join the club, but you must pay its dues. You can plant a garden, but you must tend the weeds.

---

[9] A simple example is borrowing symbols and images that one learned previously in another context. Ludwig Wittgenstein commented: "My thinking, like everyone's, has sticking to it the shriveled remains of my earlier (withered) ideas" (1980, p. 23e).

[10] Wittgenstein observed tartly that each new religion brands the old gods as devils (1980, p. 15 e).

[11] Making this project more difficult, however, is the fact that cultural changes are frequently subtle, even obscure, the better to preserve the popular sense that the world still makes sense. It is often the case that the magnitude of a change is not accompanied by the sort of drama that attracts journalists and historians. As Geertz put it: "Some of the greatest revolutions occur in the dark" (1973, p. 238). The more vivid outbursts and dislocations such as riots and war are sometimes a result of other, subterranean shifts in meaning that took place over long periods of time, without anyone necessarily even being aware that it was happening.

Leadership will frequently challenge, conserve, or renew these forms (Cassirer, 1942/2000, p. 123). Culture can be understood as the constellation of these forms and schemas and symbols (see e.g. Williams, 1894). A science of culture is, in this sense, the study of these forms and their constellation, individually and collectively, including their character, their history, and a catalog of their meanings. Such a project would do two things: *sort* the relevant phenomena – for example, these forms and constellations (Cassirer, 1946, pp. 27 & 72; see Geertz, 1973, pp. 15, 25, 91, & 93) – and also *investigate* what brought them about (Cassirer, 1942/2000, pp. 58 & 87).

The welter of preexisting cultural forms at any given time offers a wide range of possibilities. Some theorists complained about the tendency of these forms to impinge on one's freedom – which they do. Max Weber, for example, famously lamented the tendency of bureaucracy to become an iron cage (1958). The existing forms can be seen as so many hindrances to one's purpose. Other theorists, however, such as Georg Simmel, saw them as a variety of opportunities to be adopted and adapted. One has choices in life. Forms represent choices, just as one's language with all of its rules of spelling, punctuation, and grammar makes poetry possible. Human beings are not completely free to do as they like, of course, since they must contend with such realities as material scarcity, their own personal limitations, the interference of other people, and prevailing configurations of social power such as institutions. Nevertheless, these possibilities that we call "forms" represent opportunities for leadership. Leaders can be found to invoke, entrench, question, alter, and even destroy these sociological forms, conforming to one while at the same time dismantling another. This notion of a leader's interactions with such forms is one useful way of studying what leaders do.

In fact, leadership itself is a form that has a history and various meanings, capable of being revised by participants as the need arises (Harter, 2007). Leadership Studies is largely the investigation of this one form as it operates within the broader world of forms – that is, the creation, perpetuation, resistance, and ultimately transcendence into new ones. One might think of leadership as a cultural form adapted for the purpose of collectively adapting the world in some way (see Cassirer, 1942/2000, p. 50 ff.). In this sense, participants can be said to create themselves, as individuals and as collectivities (Cassirer, 1942/2000, p. 54). Geertz (1973) called human beings self-completing animals. We are agents of our own realization (p. 218). That project takes leadership. And the story of that great unfolding across time constitutes culture.

As stated, one begins in a world of preexisting cultural forms. Clifford Geertz referred to humanity as "an animal suspended in webs of significance he himself has spun" (1973, p. 5). Participants then bring something of themselves into this world; we might think of humanity's contribution as an inexhaustible restlessness or need to develop, express, and assert one's identity. As bearers of culture, they undergo some kind of experience that arrests their attention (Cassirer, 1946, pp. 32 ff., 58, & 71). It might be so abrupt and startling as to elicit no more than an exclamation, such as "wow" or "ouch." Initially, in order to remember the experience and communicate it to other people, a participant will summon an available symbol or image from the available inventory (Cassirer, 1946, pp. 36 & 38).[12] Walker Percy explained, "I cannot know anything at all unless I symbolize it" (1954–1975, p. 72). He wrote that "symbols are the vehicles of meaning" (p. 156). Participants rarely invent entirely new symbols or images; people tend to rely on the forms that already exist, even if what they do with them is meant to be unique (Cassirer, 1946, p. 44). The trick is to liberate the experience from a familiar (if not stale) vocabulary, and instead make it vivid. This decision makes sense only to the extent that the selected symbol or image can be shared with other people (Percy, 1954–1975, pp. 72 & 156).

Speaking specifically about leadership, then, that arresting experience that starts the whole process, whatever it is, might be a grievance or a fresh idea that induces a sense of purpose, no matter how vague. If there is no originating purpose, of course, there is nothing to share and no reason for leadership to begin. Likewise, if there is no other person with whom to share one's purpose – that is, a possible follower – then there will be no leadership. Furthermore, if there is no symbol or image capable of representing that originating purpose, then a leader cannot communicate anyway; he or she is as good as mute. And if the other person does not grasp the meaning of the leader's symbol or image, then the leadership will fail because the communication between them will have failed (Percy, 1954–1975, pp. 200, 256, & 259). Today, a prospective leader has almost too many possible symbols and images to choose from, especially in a global and multicultural context, with a variety of communication platforms (Cassirer, 1942/2000, p. 111). Misunderstanding is always a risk.

So far, we have considered how one makes sense of personal experience by means of culture, ultimately by capturing and transmitting meaning in symbols and images. In the next section, we will consider the problem of making sense of the symbols and images presented to us by other people.

---

[12] Clifford Geertz claimed that "meanings can only be 'stored' in symbols" (1973, p. 127). Anthony Giddens said that the meaning of a symbol or cultural form is usually thought to depend on how it was intended by the person using it, yet its meaning probably precedes its use. As he put it, the X-meaning (its cultural meaning) is prior to the S-meaning (its subjective meaning) (1993, p. 97).

2.4 Making Sense of the Symbols and Images of Others

Inspiration in leadership studies often pops up in unlikely places. The German Hans-Georg Gadamer, a gentle scholar in strenuous times and a philosopher with impeccable academic credentials, once crafted an essay that David Linge translated as "The Universality of the Hermeneutical Problem" (Gadamer, 1976). Its argument opens out onto interesting vistas for the consideration of leadership as a phenomenon, although to arrive at those vistas, one must first retrace the path that he took to get there.

In doing so, however, one will have to interpret what Gadamer was trying to say in that essay – omitting some portions, for example, and compressing others. Not that Gadamer would object in principle, inasmuch as the essay acknowledges the necessity of interpretation as a means to understanding. We actually have no choice but to interpret language if we hope to understand each other's purpose. The symbols and images must be made to yield their meaning. This practice of interpretation goes by the formal name of *hermeneutics*.

Gadamer explained in this essay that hermeneutics has been going on for millennia, especially in multiple religious traditions. From there, scholars began trying to derive meaning from other kinds of texts and artifacts – be it from literature, historical documents, works of art, or constitutions. In each case, the observer stands before some object comprised of symbols and images rendered by another human being and wonders about its purpose. That is how the process begins – in wonder.

Typically, people claim that the way to understand another person is to imagine oneself as that other person and shed whatever filters might be distorting perception. The objective would be to set aside or bracket somehow your upbringing, your culture, your historical era, and your gender or race, and instead remove your "self" in order to gain the other person's point of view. One might say that to understand me, you must empty yourself of what makes you *you*. Only then will you come to understand. That is, please try as best you can to imagine what the other person might have been thinking at the time. This is a familiar method.

Gadamer understood this approach as an ideal of objectivity, as well as understanding the motivation for it to prevent bias and distortion, although in the aforementioned essay, he decided to question not only whether it might be possible to empty oneself in this way but also whether it was even a good idea. Gaining critical distance from one's self means breaking some important bonds you have with that other person. By emptying yourself, you yourself become an abstraction – that is, an impersonal, perhaps unfeeling clinician and not a full-blooded human who feels drawn to understanding someone else in the first place. Presumably, the other person was reaching out to you *as a person*, with all of your hopes and fears and memories and desires. Why not accept that fact (contra Benjamin, 1968, p. 11)?

In the words of the social sciences, was the author (the creator and originator) desiring to be explained or to be *understood*? These are not the same thing.

Before you judge what the other person was trying to say, you presuppose that there is something to hear. You posit the message, even if you do not know what it is. Otherwise, why would you even look? You are interested in that message. You are disposed to listen. You have to believe it is there, embodied in the artifact, or you would not bother. As Steven Johnson (2001) once put it, your job is to reach around the noise to find the signal. You encounter the artifact (whatever it is) and intend to interpret it. To that extent, at the very least, you have prejudged. You are prejudiced.

For Gadamer, prejudice is not necessarily a bad thing. In fact, it is necessary. For Gadamer, prejudices are "conditions whereby we experience something" (1976, p. 9). They make experiences meaningful. Yet, we rarely become aware of these prejudices. To the extent we do become aware of them, we try to look past them or disavow them for the sake of some method of analysis (see generally Dostal, 2002; Simms, 2015). The modern natural sciences embrace this ideal of the disinterested investigator, shorn of prejudice, which for the natural sciences might be a proper position to take (cf. Polanyi, 2009). Their work produces answers to questions – questions about the universe, about life, about the constitution of being – but what Gadamer would like to know is this: What were the originating questions? Where did they come from? Questions do not float around, waiting for some technician to pluck them out of the ether. They somehow "occur" in the human mind. Often, the question already contains or embodies a set of prejudices that will influence the process. Knowing the question makes it likelier to understand the proposed answer (see Wilson, 2016).

Gadamer urged his reader to pay closer attention to the originating question. He argued that questions such as "why?" and "what if?" originate ultimately in the imagination (1976, p. 12). It was Socrates, after all, who exemplified the practice of philosophy – not as a series of assertions that methodically lead to a conclusion, step-by-step, but rather as a series of questions. Socrates was trying to *interpret* what the other person believed. Much depends, therefore, on the art of posing what Gadamer referred to as "real productive questions" (p. 12). Again, hermeneutics as a practice enables us to recognize the questions that prompted the artifact. And having done so, we are in a better position to understand what it meant. What was the other person responding to so that he or she felt compelled to say this?

Why do nations use flags? Or anthems? Or holidays? Why do businesses design logos? In other words, what a leader does (to a large extent) is to *interrogate* social reality and the symbols that we use to describe it.[13]

Gadamer was not unmindful that people do not necessarily share the same prejudices. You and I are different people. If we were not any different, there would be nothing to interpret. Nevertheless, we are in fact different. And because we are different, my interpretation of your message might not align perfectly with your purpose. We can misunderstand each other. It happens all the time. Nevertheless, what follows is a significant insight. We speak as though your purpose and my purpose are out there somewhere, fully formed and floating in our minds, so that it is just a matter of bringing them together. What Gadamer found especially exciting is that during the process of interpretation, we can also create something new that *neither of us* would have anticipated. In the space between one person and another, as they engage in this mutual process of "closing the gap" or dialogue, they can arrive at completely novel outcomes. Elsewhere, Gadamer stated: "Through every dialogue something different comes to be" (1976, p. 58). To that extent, hermeneutics can be *generative*. None of us knows in advance where the process will turn, yet it could be so much better than what either of us in isolation could have achieved. The symbol or image issued by the other person could be construed as an invitation to collaborate on shared meaning. In leadership, this is frequently the case.

When people encounter each other and engage each other – not dispassionately, as lab technicians, but as full participants from out of each of their respective webs of prejudice – the result can be maddening or delightful or utterly strange. That is the risk and promise of dialogue, even if the other person in that dialogue was a sculptor who died 2,000 years ago. We have to assume, said Gadamer, that the other person expected this kind of response from us.

Consequently, you and I might consider how to appropriate Gadamer's essay for leadership studies. Leadership is an interpersonal process, an exchange of sorts in which the participants try to understand each other (Harter, 2015). Leadership presupposes intentional change, novelty, initiative; otherwise, instinct (nature) and habit (culture) would suffice. Often, when we study leadership, we look for the behavior – that is, the speeches, the gestures, the decisions, the observable shift in conduct. For it is in those moments that we can be said to witness leadership. Otherwise, all of that activity on the part of the leader is for naught if nobody on the other end comes to agree.

---

[13] The term "interrogate" has come to mean the examination of one's assumptions or premises; to look behind something at what has been presupposed or taken for granted. Interrogation swings the scrutiny around toward that which had been tacit.

Perhaps with Gadamer we might push further back, behind the little spark that attracts so much attention, back to the originating question that framed the conversation to begin with. We might ask ourselves: "Leadership in response to what?" One understands Napoleon best in the context of the French Revolution. One understands Hitler best in the context of Weimar Germany and World War I. One understands the Reverend Dr. Martin Luther King, Jr. best in the context of Jim Crow.

What Gadamer's essay suggests to me is that my intended audience – that is, scholars and educators in leadership studies – notice where these *questions* come from. Who imagined the question to begin with? – even if it was not they who found the answer. One has to consider whether it would be leadership to frame the predicament that elicits the response? If this proves to be a fruitful line of investigation, it also raises the logical question about how we educate leaders today. Could leadership education be as much about how to recognize and frame questions as it is about finding the answer? To start down this path is to open out onto educating the imagination.

3 The Relationship between Leadership and Culture

H. Richard Niebuhr listed five possibilities for a relationship with culture, culminating in the idea that leadership and culture are reciprocal, which is to say mutually constituting. Culture constrains, enables, and shapes leadership for the purpose of external adaptation and internal integration. It provides a guide for behavior, a sense of belonging, and an expression of shared values. Culture influences what type of leadership even works. Leadership, in turn, operates within culture as a context, using it, defying it, reforming it, or maybe even creating it anew; nevertheless, the first step is simply to become aware of one's culture and obtain a vantage point from outside, for the sake of judging how people customarily do things. Leadership works to reach goals, adapting to changing circumstances and coordinating a variety of people. Sometimes, the very goal that motivates a leader is to change the culture.

3.1 Introduction

Writing in 1944, Kurt Lewin offered this advice: "Research on leadership . . . will have to be designed to reach the properties of large social units [and] has to link these data which are commonly attributed to such different sciences as sociology [and] cultural anthropology" (1944, p. 394 f.). Sixty-seven years later, Mats Alvesson has explained that – despite the "very poor consideration" in the literature of the relationship between leadership and culture – we do possess some awareness about the extent to which leadership influences culture and vice versa (2002, pp. 157–161).

The purpose of this section is to frame that relationship, beginning with a classic schema that depicts the permutations. Next, this section looks at culture as a causal mechanism, especially its impact on leadership, before looking at the broader functions that culture appears to serve. Finally, the section describes many of the ways that leadership affects culture, so that we can say the two influence one another.

3.2 Niebuhr's Five Possibilities

Perhaps it goes without saying that you can imagine the relationship between leadership and culture in different ways. Edgar Schein (2004) wrote that culture and leadership are two sides of the same coin (p. 10). Alvesson adopted the imagery of a *spectrum*, ranging from the individual social actor, at one pole, to the culture as an encompassing whole, at the other (2011, p. 154; see Kroeber & Kluckhohn, 1963, p. 361). The imagery that I prefer originates in a 1951 book by H. Richard Niebuhr called *Christ and Culture*, who suggested five different possibilities, as follows.

3.2.1 Possibility One

Niebuhr's scheme suggests that we can conceive that leadership and culture have nothing whatsoever to do with each other. Emile Durkheim, for instance, insisted that sociology would not be interested in the exertions of individual social actors (see 1895/1938). Social facts can be explained only by other social facts. Likewise, leadership and culture can be thought to occupy different levels of analysis, so that a division of labor among academics would warrant their being kept separate. That is one possibility, though it is a possibility that this Element was written to set aside, given that leadership continues to be investigated at multiple levels (Rousseau, 1985; Yammarino & Dionne, 2019; Yammarino & Gooty, 2017), including at the macro level (e.g. Ospina & Hittleman, 2011). One misperceives the nature of leadership to regard it as a distinct, micro phenomenon, or what Colvin labeled as a focus on individual outcomes only (Harter, 2020).

3.2.2 Possibility Two

We can choose to conceive that leadership and culture do have something to do with each other, but what that might be precisely will vary. For example, they can be conceived as opposing forces, struggling against one another. This oppositional relationship is possibility number two.

Often, writers treat culture as the recalcitrant raw material for leadership, in the same way that a mariner might contend with the sea. Under this imagery, culture is seen to compete against and ultimately to overwhelm leadership (Yukl, 2013, p. 165). Perhaps the best effort to analyze such a climate frustrating leadership belongs to Ralph Hummel's *The Bureaucratic Experience* (2008, ch. 3). Better known, of course, are the dystopias of George Orwell and Margaret Atwood, and their ilk. Mats Alvesson has labeled this theme "culture as constraint" (2002, ch. 6; see Fairholm, 1994, p. 44; Hofstede, 1993).

Sometimes, of course, culture does not win. Many studies of great leaders cast them as heroic figures clashing and ultimately changing or displacing an entire culture. In this scenario, the leaders are St. George and culture is the dragon. One thinks, for example, of Peter the Great and his gargantuan effort to modernize Russia (see Taylor, 1999, p. 41) – a project more or less completed by Lenin 200 years later. To succeed, of course, they had to defy, suppress, and otherwise resist the extant traditions, including serfdom and the authority of the Russian Orthodox Church. Possibility Two presents culture and leadership as adversaries.

3.2.3 Possibility Three

Another theme is that leadership can be conceived to be a product of the culture. Let us consider the fact that, to a great extent, culture does at least shape leadership. One of the purposes of the rightly famous GLOBE studies (House et al., 2004) was an investigation into the cultures from out of which leadership emerges, in part to designate what people within a given culture are likely to see as leadership and thus prefer. This approach to the study of leadership and culture can resolve itself in the extreme position, exemplified by the novelist Leo Tolstoy, who was of the opinion that even kings are the slaves of history (see Berlin, 1978). If a leader such as Napoleon did not exist, it would be necessary to create him. A more moderate view – i.e. that such extraordinary characters exist regardless of the circumstances, independent of their times – does not negate the fact that their fortunes depend on conditions. Another way of saying this is that we will always find a Caesar in our midst, but he won't really become Caesar as we understand the term until the times are ripe. Culture determines who leads and how extensively their influence will reach. That is one way to describe Possibility Three.

Culture can be said to produce the leadership that we get. Thinking back, it was an alien culture further west that informed Peter the Great, as well as

Vladimir Lenin, about the possible direction to take Russia. The culture of Western Europe shaped their leadership. But that's not all. They were each authoritarian figures reflective of a traditional affinity for such leadership. The claim is often made that Russians prefer their leadership to be solitary and absolute, extending all the way back to the great Khans perhaps, but certainly the czars (contra Blass, 1999, regarding Milgram experiments). That is to say, the Russians and their far-flung empire were themselves conditioned by centuries to being governed by a lone and dictatorial ruler – so much so that part of Lenin's appeal was that he embodied the ideal that Nicholas II had failed to reach. Accordingly, we might say that Peter and Lenin were produced by two rival cultures. But is that a sufficient explanation? They also worked *against* aspects of these two cultures.

3.2.4 Possibility Four

After seeing that to some extent culture produces leadership, we can also recognize that leadership produces culture. A number of writers on leadership have taken this position, namely that culture belongs to and arises out of leadership. One could use the example of Peter the Great (and Lenin) as evidence for this approach, inasmuch as the fact of Russia having become modern is attributable to the singular exertions of these men. It strains credulity to think that this would have happened otherwise. But then, entrepreneurs and civic founders always preside at the inception. Leaders sometimes literally create a culture. Once a culture is underway, reformers are often celebrated for shifting the trajectory in one direction or another. Edgar Schein makes these possibilities the very purpose of leadership. Possibility Four is that leadership exists to create, manage, and possibly alter a culture (2004, p. 11; e.g. Trice & Beyer, 1991 f; cf. Alvesson, 1993, ch. 5).

Within this theme, one might claim that in the absence of leadership, culture has a kind of inertia, extending itself indefinitely and possibly adrift. Scholars can describe a culture as though it is a static phenomenon because for long stretches of time, a culture persists in a recognizable form. Things get interesting, however, when a culture is transformed. And it strains the imagination that a culture transforms itself spontaneously, in the complete absence of leadership.[14]

---

[14] Nevertheless, we do have to be prepared for that possibility. Manuel de Landa gives the example of long vowel sounds in English that over the course of several generations "slid" as a group with no evidence of agency on anyone's part (2000, p. 209 f., quoting Bryson, 1990). Sometimes, he claims, a system evolves on its own, according to internal laws, whether anybody wants it to or not. This is not a trivial assertion.

3.2.5 Possibility Five

So far, we have considered four possibilities (A and B are unrelated; A and B are opposing; A produces B; B produces A). The fifth and most satisfying possibility is to conceive of them as separate things conceptually that are engaged with each other, mutually influencing each other. Perhaps we can say that leadership and culture are reciprocal: they hold one another in a dynamic tension. Neither A nor B has to have preeminence. Each presupposes the other. And the nature of their relationship might be manifest on occasion as *opposition* (Possibility Two), or as one *producing* the other (Possibilities Three and Four), but then from a transcending point of view, they simply interact reciprocally, back and forth. Both A and B participate in something comprehending them both, which we might think of as C. Under this fifth possibility, therefore, insisting on any of the previous four themes might be useful for limited purposes, but ultimately that would be reductionist and limiting.

As Terry Eagleton was to put it: "Human beings are not mere products of their environs, but neither are those environs sheer clay for their arbitrary self-fashioning" (2000, p. 5; see Alvesson, 1993, p. 31 Moody-Adams, 1997, p. 83). In 1970, Robert Merton addressed this sense of reciprocity as part of the "ambivalence of organizational leaders," where he quoted Winston Churchill as follows: "We shape our organizations and afterwards our organizations shape us" (1976, p. 77). This is succinctly said and reminiscent of the position held by Georg Simmel, which we had reason to mention in the previous section.

Keen observers know that it goes both ways. Leaders form, change, reproduce, and maintain culture, according to Alvesson, but then culture defines and constrains leadership, even setting standards for what constitutes leadership in the first place, let alone good leadership.[15] In this regard, Alvesson echoes well-established findings in anthropology (see Kroeber & Kluckhohn, 1963, p. 179). There, a circularity of influence has been accepted: that is, we know that people shape their culture, but then culture shapes the people (Kroeber & Kluckhohn, 1963, p. 326).

Other factors influencing the composition of any culture include biological variation, the physical environment, and processes of history (Kroeber & Kluckhohn, 1963, p. 350; cf. Benedict, 1934/2005, pp. 233–236). The causes of culture are complex and difficult to untangle (Kroeber & Kluckhohn, 1963, p. 326). At the center of anthropological study, however, are the activities of its

---

[15] That is to say, what in one context would be regarded as effective leadership would hardly be noticed at all in another context. Den Hartog and Dickson not only concur (2004, p. 250f), they also write about something called a culture's Implicit Leadership Theory, or CLT (p. 269).

inhabitants. And obviously among its inhabitants would be leaders. Culture can be understood therefore as a product of human action, a condition for further action, and a causal factor in its own right (Kroeber & Kluckhohn, 1963, p. 357).

3.3 Culture's Impact on Leadership

What does it mean to say that culture produces or constrains, as though it is itself a causal agent? We must be careful ascribing agency to a culture (Alvesson, 1993, pp. 41–43), as though it is an independent social actor. Perhaps it is a useful fiction.

Investigators wanting to incorporate notions of culture into their studies of leadership often write about the way that culture influences leaders. In one sense, we talk about culture as an enveloping medium for our individual behavior, the environment to our systems, in the same way that we talk about the "playing conditions" in athletics or about the "timing" for the launch of a new enterprise or the "era" in which a painter emerges. Culture from this point of view is the milieu for what ostensibly interests us in leadership studies, like the ocean within which the fish are found to swim. The culture tends to frame what can or cannot happen. Priests would consult the auguries in order to determine whether the stars or the gods are auspicious. In the same manner, a prudent pilot consults the weather, an entrepreneur scans the market, a candidate for public office polls the electorate. For understandable reasons, leadership stands in relation to culture as the figure to the ground. From this point of view, if leadership is the chalk, culture is the chalkboard. If leadership is the goldfish, culture is the fishbowl. I happen to believe that this imagery of figure and ground is unduly limiting. Let me explain.

Culture also has a different role, however. It is more than the medium within which we all swim. Perhaps in accordance with the wishes of Durkheim, we often speak as though culture possesses its own agency – a vague and broad impersonal force, frequently personified and blamed in the same way that a cab driver complains about the traffic. The word "culture" is in these instances intended to embody a myriad of elements and treat them as a unified social actor, with purpose and responsibility. We often speak as though culture makes things happen or prevents things from happening (contra Moody-Adams, 1997, p. 95).

This is in many ways not unlike our practice of naming hurricanes. From a systems perspective, anything to which we assign a name and to which we ascribe agency is itself a multiplicity, a configuration of elements that are themselves discovered to be subsystems in and of themselves (Meadows, 2008). In other words, one could argue that culture possesses agency in the same way that leaders possess agency – only to a greater magnitude. In any case, it is not altogether clear in what way culture possesses agency as a separate social actor, despite the fact that we frequently talk as though it does.

3.4 Functions of Culture

By now, we have begun to see culture as something to be represented in a *static model*, enumerating its elements and explaining the relationships among these elements. This treats culture as a thing, an object, with at least somewhat discernible dimensions. Part of that static model is culture as a collection or array of products, which includes both tangible artifacts and intangible representations or symbols for prescribed meanings. In addition, Faulkner et al. also adopt a *dynamic model*, with culture itself as a process (2006, pp. 40–43). Culture is something that happens, including the following: differentiating ourselves from other peoples, establishing hierarchies, and making sense of the world. But why do this? Culture wouldn't persist if there was not a set of *functions* that culture performs. Here lies another way to represent culture: not what culture is, so much as what culture does (Faulkner et al., 2006, pp. 38–40) – things such as guiding or controlling behavior, providing a sense of belonging and identity to members, and expressing values and feelings. The idea of a culture does tend to separate *us* from *them*. You and I have our culture. It is this that we have in common. Culture is one way that we tell one another apart (Hofstede, Hofstede, & Minkov, 2010, pp. 6, 12 ff., & 17; Ortega y Gasset, 1957, p. 111).

So long as we are looking at functions that culture performs, two of them are especially relevant to the study of leadership. Deanne Den Hartog and Marcus Dickson (2004) added the following distinction: some of the fundamental problems to be solved by means of culture have to do with (a) external *adaptation* – that is, responding to the environment – whereas some have to do with (b) internal *integration* – that is, getting organized. In either case, culture provides a pattern for response (see also Schein, 2004, p. 18). "That's just how we do things around here." Culture provides the heuristics by which we cope. Because culture conveniently supplies a rough-and-ready response, participants waste little cognitive energy trying to figure out what to do next (Den Hartog & Dickson, 2004, p. 269). The template is already available. What this suggests is that culture provides substitutes for leadership (see Kerr & Jermier, 1978), because if we have a way of doing things already, we shouldn't need leaders. Thus, culture exists in part to make leadership unnecessary, if not unwelcome. But then, to be thorough, the way that culture does these things may be by means of leadership. In this sense, leadership is adjunct to culture, a mechanism by which culture adapts and integrates.

Thus, "cultures consist of structures and processes that serve a variety of functions" (Hecht, Baldwin, & Faulkner, 2006, p. 67).[16] In summary, then, functional understandings of culture explain what it does and why it exists. Among the functions relative to leadership are adaptation to the environment (out there) and integration or organization (in here) (Schein, 2004, p. 16). The theologian Emil Brunner laid out a charming enumeration of culture's myriad functions.

> The impulse to create the beautiful, to realise justice, to know the truth, to preserve the past, to enter into spiritual communication, to invent the new, to extend the range of human intercommunication, to share the sufferings and joys of others; the impulse to submit the totality of life to ultimate directives and give it a meaning, unity and intelligibility, and finally to place everything under the divine will. (1949, p. 128)

Cooper (2020) traces this way of thinking back to Aristotle, who distinguished between (a) utilitarian motives, such as obtaining food and shelter, and (b) the wonder that arises when contemplating the cosmos. One might wish to *control* something useful such as fire, but you wish to *connect with* the stars in an act of imaginative participation (2020, p. 80 f.). Human beings adapt the world around them, to the extent that they can, but they also adapt themselves to it, deriving meaning in terms of a comprehending order.

Brunner acknowledged that participants in these same activities of imaginative participation can be influenced by egoism, lust for power, and ambition. This fact can turn culture into something ridiculous or horrifying as people try to adapt that to which they are meant to be adapted. Why is that? One requires a point of reference from outside of one's culture by which to judge (1949, p. 131). Among the points of reference from which to judge culture are the family, the human body (including its health), the rule of law, tradition, and religion (1949, pp. 133–136). A leader can assess a given culture from one or more of these perspectives. And in Brunner's opinion, the reverse is not true. One must not use culture to judge the family, health, law, tradition, or religion – for, in that instance, culture would have exceeded its proper bounds. That is as much to say that culture may be aspirational but perhaps it should not be regulative. Except that in fact, for many people, it does serve to regulate everything else. Brunner understood this as a regrettable reality.

We might say that leadership can aid in the functions that culture serves, such as adaptation and integration, but it should also probably represent a point of

---

[16] Alvesson listed a number of additional metaphors (1993, pp. 16–24).

reference outside of that culture, an Archimedean point from which to critique or judge that culture (Harter, 2020). Therefore, leadership can serve as this imaginative participation in the cosmos to which humans must adapt themselves if their lives are to have meaning. Leaders should have the capacity to transcend their culture, from a critical perspective, despite the necessity of using that culture – its symbols and practices – to bring about change.

3.5 Leadership's Impact on Culture

From the point of view of the leader, then, what should be the posture one takes with regard to the prevailing culture? Obviously, one has a range of options. Leaders can obey, perpetuate, embed, transmit, question, challenge, defy, evade, reform, reject, leave, and in rare cases create entirely out of nothing. This is only an illustrative list. Given the complex and inconsistent nature of culture at different levels of abstraction, a leader can obey one part while rejecting another. A leader can defy the encompassing culture at the macro level by fostering a new heterodox culture at the micro level. A leader can resist certain norms or practices as inconsistent with paramount claims – as Martin Luther King, Jr. did. In other words, the leader can be doing all of these things and doing them simultaneously.

The posture one might take, therefore, begins with *awareness* (Schein, 2004, p. 23). Leaders must notice the keys, codes, and cues to effective social action – and this includes sitting in judgment of them as well. A leader may ask whether the culture is in fact internally consistent, coherent, and clear – and where is it not. Is there a conflict brewing? Is it possible that a hidden variable has previously escaped notice? Schein wrote that "if elements of a culture become dysfunctional, it is the unique function of leadership to be able to perceive the functional and dysfunctional elements of the existing culture and to manage cultural evolution and change" (2004, p. 22 f.). Regardless of the purpose, as Fairholm noted, "[t]he key to making cultural change is to understand the existing culture" (1994, p. 55). Toward this end, David Livermore (2015) has emphasized what he calls Cultural Intelligence, or CQ. Learn the extent to which culture is shaping you, as well as the extent to which you are shaping the culture. Having said that, nobody can fully grasp the contents of a culture. Culture is just too big and complex and rife with inconsistency. We are talking about a matter of degree. Which features are relevant? Which way do they cut? Could there be countervailing forces at work within the culture?

By participating in any culture, to some extent, one is perpetuating it, reinforcing its values, even if only tacitly. To participate is to perpetuate. Often, that is precisely what leadership has been instituted to accomplish –

that is, to uphold, exemplify, and reinforce the prevailing culture. Fairholm referred to this task as cultural maintenance (1994, p. 69). But of course leaders also alter culture. It is not the case that the ultimate purpose of leadership is simply to reconcile cultural inconsistencies and render a culture more coherent, reinforcing its internal structures, making it in any sense "tighter" (see Gelfand, 2019). The reason is that a consistent and coherent culture can also be dysfunctional or immoral (Wang et al., 2021).

Kroeber and Kluckhohn conceded that "culture change could not occur were it not for the creative activity of concrete individuals," such that you need to understand these exertions in order to develop "a satisfactory theory of cultural phenomena" (1963, p. 213; see also Benedict, 1934/2005, p. 253). This might sound like an opening for leadership studies. Yet, leadership cannot explain all of it (Kroeber & Kluckhohn, 1963, pp. 290 & 361). Benedict points out that whereas individuals do make contributions to culture, many if not most people "shape to the form of their culture" and "are plastic to the moulding force of the society [and] take quite readily the form that is presented to them" (1934/2005, p. 254 f.). That is, they are passive when it comes to culture and to a great extent are products of the culture, whether they know it or not. Individuals can make a difference, she concedes. It is just that not many of them do. And of those who do, they do not make much of a difference.

Leaders often work within a given culture, using it to achieve a purpose. One might think of this as an instrumental approach. They wear the uniform and sing the songs. The story is told that the wife of a prominent politician knew that her husband was running for president of the United States when he insisted that the family start going to church. He had brought himself and his family into alignment with the culture of the time. By way of contrast, within a given culture, leaders might gain attention by defiance or otherwise setting themselves apart, gaining notoriety by making an exception of themselves. Alcibiades studiously differentiated himself from his peers (Plutarch, 2001). So also did the pharaoh Akhenaten (Mahfouz, 1985/2000). Likewise, some leaders already present themselves as exceptions to the prevailing culture by coming in from outside of the community (e.g. Schein, 2004, pp. 306–309; Simmel, 1908/1950). Yet, leaders also work not only *within* a culture but also *on* culture, consciously trying to alter it in some fashion.

Here is another attempt to explain the relationship between leadership and culture. Robert Colvin (1996) cited Parsons (1960) to the effect that leadership consists of working to obtain goals, adapting to changing circumstances in the pursuit of those goals, and coordinating a variety of people to do these things with you. Furthermore, leaders (and especially executive leaders) have a responsibility to foster a culture that facilitates these three tasks (p. 115).

Leaders are responsible for cultural outcomes. Toward that end, Colvin distinguished cultural outcomes from individual outcomes, almost as though they are macro and micro. Leadership can in fact impact either or both. He explained that individual outcomes can subsequently become causal factors at the cultural level regarding the prevailing vision, values, and ideas (pp. 5 & 117). By influencing other people, you can influence the culture (p. 18, figure 2). An example might be consistently rewarding employees individually for a job well done, thereby retaining good workers and contributing to a culture of stability, with less turnover. Colvin went on to say that not only is this possible, it is frankly necessary, especially in a broad and diverse context requiring unification around a shared purpose (pp. 86 & 90).

At any given point in time, a culture will recognize certain individual persons as leaders – for example, those who preside, enforce, and educate. These leaders may not always agree with one another, and in fact they might be working at cross-purposes. Nevertheless, together, they constitute an elite entrusted with the perpetuation of that culture (e.g. Pareto, 1901/1991). Simultaneously, leaders arise to thwart and challenge the culture – or to draw participants in that culture away to another way of living (e.g. Moses). The study of leadership encompasses each of these social actors.

3.6 Concluding Thoughts

Leadership and culture are mutually constituting. Over time, they influence one another. Culture serves as a backdrop to individual exertions, but often culture makes leadership possible, if not necessary. Leaders also *use* culture to achieve their aims. All of these things could be happening at one and the same time. The relationship between the two is dynamic, complex, and unending. They are so entwined, one with the other, that leadership scholars might not know where to begin their studies. The next section offers a place to start, accompanied by an historical example.

Perhaps the obvious thing should not go unsaid. When investigating any particular, concrete episode, students of leadership will want to examine the interplay between leadership and culture. Happily, we know that leadership can influence culture, in myriad ways. In order to do so, leaders must step outside of the prevailing culture that shaped them, gaining critical distance in order to judge what might need to be upheld and preserved, on the one hand, and what might need to be scrapped or altered, on the other. Many resources in the literature already exist that explain how to do this, which it would be impossible to summarize here. In addition to the foremost scholars already identified, such as Schein, Hofstede, and House, for example, plenty of popular authors have weighed in on how to do this.[17] Speaking in broad terms, leaders can in fact use a culture to bring about change to that culture. Furthermore, the goal would be a new, perhaps revised culture. At a higher level of abstraction, a leader might consider what kind of leadership the resulting culture will subsequently foster, which is as much as to say that leaders might consider designing cultures that foster improved leadership in the future (see e.g. Manz & Sims, 1991). Even then, leaders cannot do this alone. They must collaborate with others, as the next section will illustrate.

4 The Cultural Phenomenon of the King James Bible, 1611

José Ortega y Gasset suggested the unit of analysis for cultural change to be the generation. At any time, a culture includes elements of the past, the present, and possible futures. Each generation has a choice whether to adopt the culture as transmitted to them or to adapt it to their values. Most members of a given generation adopt the culture handed to them, but a small group of likeminded peers can set out to alter the culture completely. One historical example would be the collective project in England of translating the Holy Bible into the vernacular, formally organized under King James to account for Protestant sympathies, emerging scholarship across Europe about various languages, and the pent-up demand among laypersons for printed materials. The project was not the result of any singular personality or brilliant linguist. Instead, the work was done by committees during a veritable Golden Age in English literature.

4.1 Introduction

José Ortega y Gasset pointed out some time ago that culture is presupposed to be social. Individuals acting alone rarely change a culture all by themselves. Part of a culture's moral force comes from the belief that it reflects the desires and expectations of the collective, so that individual deviance will be frowned upon, or at best ignored. Yet, deviance does happen, all the time and in all sorts of ways. Somehow, cultures do change. But how?

This section looks at the idea of the generation as the relevant social unit for studying cultural dynamics. After outlining what Ortega y Gasset meant by this, the section introduces a concrete example of a generation that changed its prevailing culture deeply, for centuries to come.

Culture does not stand still. Plainly, it participates in the flow of history. To a great extent, culture is history. Thus, a static model of culture would have limited use. It was Aristotle, if you recall, who noted that understanding means

---

[17] In 2021 alone, see e.g. Freedman; Oakes; and van Cleve.

to understand why something exists. What are its antecedents? In other words, what are the conditions for its coming to be? What caused it to emerge in just this way? Students require a dynamic model of culture. But not just any model. Archer had proffered a three-step model of cultural conditioning (as an antecedent), sociocultural interaction, and then cultural elaboration to describe the subsequent implications (1996, p. xxiv). Edmund Husserl recognized that a phenomenon such as culture is not a single thing on a simple timeline proceeding from antecedents and resulting in consequences, in the way that for geometry three points on a plane define a line. Culture participates in multiple, independent timelines and represents their confluence (see Steinbock, 1998, 2003). Biological life or genetics, material life or economics, spiritual life or religion, civic life or politics – culture emerges from a turbulence, a watercourse comprised of multiple streams. Culture is the product of histories, in the plural. Archer did point out that at any given point T_1, a culture would bear the features of at least three phases simultaneously: past, present, and possible futures (1996, p. xxv). Not everything from the past has perished, and not everything from the future has arrived. Not only does culture lie at a point of intersection for multiple histories, it actually includes multiple points of intersection. Today (T_1) contains residue from the past and harbingers of the future all mixed together. How does one make sense of these dynamics?

4.2 The Idea of the Generation

Ortega y Gasset made the case that the social unit appropriate for studying cultural leadership is the generation (1933/1961, p. 15). Each generation receives a culture from prior generations (the past). He wrote that society "already has its own interpretation of life, its repertory of ideas, of ruling convictions about the universe" (1958, p. 26). Elsewhere, he wrote, "I live among interpretations of reality which my social environment and human tradition have been inventing and accumulating. Of these, some deserve to be regarded as genuine [when] in fact, the vast majority ... are ... illusory" (1957, p. 98). Even so, this culture has a certain force. Emerging adults must learn to account for it (1958, p. 39). But they must also struggle to express themselves in creative ways, moving against or at least outside of the received culture (1933/1961, p. 16). This turn, he said, defines the unique mission for each generation: after your elders hand you their culture, such as it is, what do you preserve and what do you revise? If you and your peers rebel completely against the culture as a whole, you make yourselves vulnerable largely by ignoring the accumulated wisdom of your forbearers. You lose a sense of identity that culture provides. But if you accept the culture completely, uncritically, then you offend your calling and squander your powers. You become little more than stewards. Ortega y Gasset remarked that "ordinarily we live installed, too safely installed, within the security of our habitual, inherited, topical ideas" (1958, p. 78).

Ortega y Gasset was not naïve. He did not mean that when culture changes, the entire generation must participate. The majority of people in a given generation will not play any role whatsoever in cultural dynamics. Most are those who "demand nothing special of themselves, but for whom to live is to be every moment what they already are, without imposing on themselves any effort towards perfection; mere buoys that float on the waves" (Ortega y Gasset, 1932, p. 15). Instead, there will be only a minority, an elite, some club, brotherhood, or secret cabal that will collaborate to make things happen.[18] Many of their peers will ignore the effort or even resist. The majority will come along, likely grudging the changes. So, studying cultural leadership requires identifying that small unit of creative allies and examining their activities as a group. And their disruptive influence shows the wisdom in accepting Archer's dictum that the present always contains both the past and possible futures piled on top of one another, simultaneously competing.

Just to be clear, therefore, in the study of cultural dynamics, one does not lump everybody born at the same time together, such as the Baby Boomers or Millennials, and give them all of the credit or all the blame for what transpires. That's not how the causal mechanism works. Most folks will have been irrelevant to the process. This was as true for the Age of Enlightenment as for the Beat Generation. Having a label such as Baby Boomers does not mean that that specific generation even had a distinctive impact on social change. The label is an empty marker that says at most that this cohort is in fact a generation. And that's about all that it says. Changes to the culture belong to "a small minority of spiritual scouts, vigilant souls, who had a glimmering of distant tracts of territory still to be invaded" (Ortega y Gasset, 1933/1961, p. 12). Here among these innovators, inheritors of a shared culture, is a place for leadership.

The process begins with the selection of a point of view, the perspective that a small coterie of attentive youth adopts with regard to the prevailing culture (Ortega y Gasset, 1933/1961, p. 60). In quiescent eras, the brightest and best embrace the culture that was handed to them and seek to assimilate, developing their mastery of agreed upon goods and values. They capitalize on existing systems to get ahead. They accept the basic rules of the game. Looking at such

---

[18] Ortega y Gasset would describe this elite and its historic mission in his most famous work, *The Revolt of the Masses* (1932). It is interesting to note that Max Weber had once written, "The 'principle of the small number,' i.e., the superior political maneuverability of *small* leading groups, always dominates political activity" (quoted in Diggins, 1996, p. 70).

a generation from the *longue durée*, we might label it a precursor generation or a follower generation – or both (Ortega y Gasset, 1958, p. 62). Many generations have little or no appreciable impact on the culture. Or their impact is negligible, like taste in music or clothing fashions. In turbulent eras, by way of contrast, these same young people might reject portions of their patrimony and go in search of something more authentic. Once they do so, they find themselves in liminal space, betwixt and between, as they know to some extent what they are leaving but have not yet seen where they are going, because it is they who are building it (Ortega y Gasset, 1933/1961, p. 79). Sometimes, their efforts swing toward utopian enterprises and abstract ideals (e.g. King Arthur and the Round Table). Other times, though, they fall into disillusionment, even cynicism (e.g. the Algonquin Round Table). Much depends therefore on the shared point of view as they begin.

What causes one generation to rise up and bring about change? If, as we stated previously, leadership and culture are mutually constituting, shaping one another, then there is no point isolating them in an attempt to answer this question – a similar question to "what came first, the chicken or the egg?" Both culture and leadership combine to create what we might call a consequential generation. Even so, leaders can encourage, even foment change, no matter when they live, and when the conditions are right, they might find themselves altering the world significantly. Ascribing cultural change to one, lone social actor whom we label as a leader is probably unwise and inaccurate. Leadership is a process in which many participate, and they participate together. This, I believe, is what Ortega y Gasset intended by the term "generation."

Using words such as "revolt" or "rebellion" does not have to imply a political struggle. In many ways, the political struggle manifests a deeper struggle at the level of ideas. Even then, not every rebellion against the norm succeeds (e.g. Ortega y Gasset, 1957, p. 252). Many have unintended consequences, if they have any consequences at all (Merton, 1976, ch. 8). Nevertheless, occasionally, a minority turns what they are doing – what they value and practice – into a social force, a usage, a binding observance (Ortega y Gasset, 1957, p. 210). It is this process that Ortega y Gasset had set out to explain.

Louis Menand (2001) did a brilliant job describing such a phenomenon at Harvard University immediately after America's Civil War. Here were the scions of a peacetime elite, brought into close proximity to one another to get an education. Immediately, they all recognized two scandals that their fathers and professors were handling poorly: one of these was the war itself, a calamity by any measure; the other was the publication of Charles Darwin's theories on natural selection. The more they talked late into the night, these young men discovered (or fabricated) a response known to us today as Pragmatism. Menand went on to show that as a result of their exchanges back in college, American institutions changed slowly as the postwar culture was shifting, such that their particular philosophy came to dominate the American experience all the way into the presidency of Franklin Roosevelt some seventy years later (see e.g. Beran, 2021). They had adopted a shared point of view that transcended the antebellum consensus.

Ortega y Gasset insisted that transitions of this sort originate not in material conditions (Marx) or subconscious drives (Freud) but instead in the minds – the conscious decisions – of an energetic clique (1933/1961, pp. 101 & 131). Brought up within a tradition that they judge to be unsatisfactory, they consult one another openly, rationally (p. 103). That is, they *think* about their situation. Others born at the same time in the same predicament might succumb or flail or wreak havoc, but those who successfully change the culture use their minds. For him, therefore, the timeline of greatest significance in cultural dynamics would be philosophical.

Ortega y Gasset was quick to point out, however, that rationality alone is not enough. Very bright people with vivid imaginations can concoct all sorts of wild and fantastic schemes. And the rational mind can be the source of utopias. Often, a fanatical circle dedicated to its perfectly rational schemes will spiral into dystopia (e.g. Dostoevsky, 1871–1872/2008). But the changes that endure, the ones that seem to survive the forces of reaction, tend to function more as adjustments or adaptations (Ortega y Gasset, 1933/1961, p. 110). The novelty that they come up with might be stunning – a clean break from the past – but life's imperatives set constraints on what can be done. And as people see that the novelty actually enhances their lives, they are less likely to resist. Ortega y Gasset was adamant that cultural changes serve the purposes of living, or they won't last. He wrote, "Certain phenomena of life are selected as possible forms of culture; but of these possible forms of culture life, in its turn, selects the only ones which are suitable for future realization" (1933/1961, p. 150). That is, Ortega y Gasset fell back to say that in cultural dynamics, the impact of rationality ultimately becomes absorbed into the broader flow of practical life. Otherwise, it probably amounts to nothing of cultural significance. A generation changes its culture by orienting its thinking in ways that ultimately work.[19]

Ortega y Gasset offered his own example by citing the work of Albert Einstein, whose breakthrough publications at the time were quite recent. Ortega y Gasset judged Einstein to be proposing a fresh vision of reality that

---

[19] John Graham (1994) examined the extent to which Ortega y Gasset's philosophy could be labeled pragmatic.

could be understood by only a few intellectuals of his generation; yet, because it promised to improve human lives, Ortega y Gasset predicted that his work would eventually seep into the culture (1933/1961, pp. 135–152). And it has. History is replete with examples of generational change, ranging from the Clapham Sect in Great Britain to the second-wave feminists between 1960 and 1980. Harold Leavitt and Jean Lipman-Blumen (1995) captured this idea of the small cluster of activists in their explanation of so-called hot groups.

Some of these notable groups are not quite what Ortega y Gasset was describing, so it pays to make a few important distinctions. Some are groups only to the extent that a number of acolytes promote the brilliant teachings of a sage or guru. One thinks for example of the students of Leo Strauss or aficionados of Ayn Rand, or the psychoanalysts who apply the theories of Sigmund Freud. Another misleading grouping would be the coincidence of several prominent scholars or artists who happened to live in the same place at the same time and engaged one another separately, without the so-called *we feeling* of belonging to the same association (Ross, 1919). Their relationships were less collaborative, whether they were connected as mentor–protégé or as rivals. One thinks for example of Socrates, Plato, Aristotle, Aeschylus, Sophocles, and Euripides in ancient Athens. Or of Leonardo da Vinci, Michelangelo, and Raphael in Renaissance Florence.[20]

Nobody denies the cultural significance of these historical figures, but Ortega y Gasset was trying to describe the social mechanism for cultural change. For him, responsibility for cultural change must be seen to be both distributed and intentional. No one person created surrealism, for example. One must account for Guillaume Apollinaire, Jean Cocteau, André Breton, Max Ernst, Salvador Dalí, René Magritte, and Georges Bataille (among others). Nevertheless, they came to see themselves as working together toward a shared vision. In the same manner, English Romantic poetry belongs to such luminaries as William Wordsworth, Samuel Taylor Coleridge, John Keats, Percy Shelley, William Blake, and Lord Byron. Even when they may have quarreled, they understood themselves to be moving in the same basic direction. Ortega y Gasset had written, "A generation is an integrated manner of existence" (1958, p. 45). Another such grouping, this time from politics rather than the arts, might be the founding fathers in postcolonial America.

---

[20] Ortega y Gasset regarded the Renaissance as a confused time, a precursor to the cultural change that was imminent. The Renaissance of Leonardo, Michelangelo, and Raphael represents only the letting go of the past – and more specifically, letting go of the Middle Ages. The actual turn in European culture toward the Modern Age, he asserted, took place with Descartes and Galileo (see 1958, pp. 72 & 85). But then, he believed that art always swims ahead of the revolution (1958, p. 88).

It is my purpose in the next portion of this section to illustrate how another so-called generation participated in these complex cultural dynamics in a surprisingly understated fashion. One can barely detect in this example the influence of conventional leadership.

4.3 The King James Bible: An Example of the Generation

Robert Carroll and Stephen Prickett recently made this simple claim: "The Bible is the basic book of our civilization" (2008, p. xi). And for those who speak English, the most significant translation historically is *The Authorized Version of the Bible in English* (frequently known as the King James Bible, King James Version, or KJV). Other versions of the Christian scriptures, they wrote, remain in its shadow (2008, p. xxix). Adam Nicolson went so far as to say that this particular translation "can lay claim to be the greatest work in prose ever written in English" (2005, p. xi). David Norton asserts that the KJV is "the most important book in English religion and culture [with] a unique place ... in linguistic and literary consciousness" (2011, pp. 1 & 189; see Bragg, 2011, ch. 1). Americans certainly credit it with shaping their earliest religious sensibilities, political ideals, and literature (Campbell, 2010, p. 238; see generally Alter, 2010; Bragg, 2011, ch. 6).[21] Strange, therefore, that so little is known of its creation leading up to the year 1611 CE (see Nicolson, 2005, p. xi; Norton, 2011).

For context, the time of the Protestant Reformation, which was roughly 1517–1648 CE, accompanied a movement to translate the Christian Bible into various European vernaculars (see Harter, 2017). At the same time, we witness the emergence of the nation-state (politics) and the proliferation of mass printing (technology), each of which contributed to the pressures to change. In addition, factional struggles – especially in the United Kingdom – shaped the desire to distribute versions of the Bible that aligned with their respective doctrines – Catholic, Anglican, or Reformed (religion). That is to say that certain broad trends in European history were converging. These are among the general antecedents to change.

More specific antecedents for translating the Bible into English went back centuries. After a period of uncertainty, the KJV became the undisputed standard for centuries in the English-speaking world, even though it was itself not the first attempt to make such a translation. It had been preceded by quite a few other attempts. In 735 CE, for instance, the Venerable Bede had made

---

[21] One author called the KJV an "emblem of national identity" that constituted cultural appropriation by the British, which in turn was foisted on its far-flung colonies. The KJV was intended to unify Protestant Britain, but R. S. Sugirtharajah considers it otherwise divisive (2011, p. 147).

considerable progress (Bobrick, 2001, p. 51 f.). King Athelstan (c. 895–939 CE), the first king of England, supposedly tried to get the job done. John Wycliffe, who lived in the fourteenth century, had publicly championed the cause in England (McGrath, 2001, p. 19; but see p. 21; see generally Bobrick, 2001, ch. 1), though Wycliffe's exertions were not without furor.[22] A version wasn't completed until William Tyndale made the effort in 1525, with the first complete Bible arriving in 1535 (McGrath, 2001, pp. 315, 68–89).

As McGrath explains, "Powerful vested interests were . . . stacked up against the production of an English Bible. English kings and bishops feared that this might cause the English people to rise in revolt, and overthrow them" (McGrath, 2001, p. 22) – not unlike what appeared to have happened over in Saxony. These fears were not unfounded (pp. 52 & 65). "The religious establishment spoke Latin and French; English was the language of its political opponents" (p. 32). The powers that be (in politics, the Church, and academe) were content with this social and linguistic bifurcation until the reign of King Henry V (pp. 29 & 35).[23] For reasons such as this, S. J. Greenslade tells us, the Tyndale offering was officially prohibited and burned publicly, and everyone associated in its manufacture and sale were threatened with charges of heresy. Tyndale himself died at the stake (1963, pp. 142–147).

The times did change, of course. The culture shifted not long after Tyndale's martyrdom, as the nation's international status rose (McGrath, 2001, pp. 25 & 34), but not until efforts to suppress the earliest versions as being "too Lutheran" faltered (e.g. Greenslade, 1963, p. 145; McGrath, 2001, pp. 80–89). The culture was soon to turn on its axle.

Several lesser forays into translation now popped up (Greenslade, 1963, pp. 147–155; Norton, 2011, ch. 1), but the first successful new translations evaded the political establishment in England by being printed elsewhere and imported, at first as contraband (McGrath, 2001, p. 66). The so-called Geneva Bible, for example, came from the labor of Protestants living and working elsewhere, in a hotbed of scholarship on the continent, where they drew inspiration and ideas from John Calvin, Theodore Beza, and texts being written in French and Italian (Greenslade, 1963, p. 155 f.).

---

[22] Bobrick recounts the hubbub at Wycliffe's arraignment, with armed retainers arrayed on both sides, squabbling over whether Wycliffe could sit during the proceedings, until a spokesman shouted that he would drag the presiding bishop by his hair and throw him out of the chamber, at which point there was violence (Bobrick, 2001, p. 41).

[23] In another historical irony, the times called for a greater study of the Bible in its original languages and not English, yet the increase in scholars competent in Hebrew, Aramaic, and Greek created a brain trust that would later contribute to making the English translations with greater competence (McGrath, 2001, p. 71).

Only after considerable political intrigue did the way become clear for English Bibles to be printed in England (McGrath, 2001). Eventually, in a complete reversal that took many decades, the printing of an English Bible became a patriotic act, with accompanying imagery of the king bestowing the scripture upon his grateful people (McGrath, 2001, p. 98).[24] Even then, with the way clear to publishing in the vernacular, the struggle over different *versions* of the Bible (and their published interpretations) reflected a continuing struggle between the Anglican and Puritan understandings, with the Douay–Rheims version also emerging to represent a Roman Catholic perspective (Greenslade, 1963, pp. 161–163).

By this point, a bishop by the name of Richard Bancroft groused, "If every man's humour should be followed, there would be no end of translating" (quoted in Greenslade, 1963, p. 164). Consequently, once King James assumed the throne in 1603, he tried to thread the needle, as it were, and put a stop to the bewildering variety by authorizing one version, once and for all. If there were to be struggles, he reasoned, they could take place on the learned committees where the translation was to be hammered out. And so it began, among both Anglicans and Puritans who shared an animus against any Roman Catholic influence in England (McGrath, 2001, p. 163). In this sense, one of the precipitating causes of the cultural shift that was about to occur was James I's desire as monarch to unify the realm.

The committees were charged to borrow heavily from previous efforts, including those of Wycliffe and Tyndale (Bobrick, 2001, p. 238; Greenslade, 1963, p. 165; McGrath, 2001, pp. 176–178). The preface stated: "We never thought to make a new translation, nor yet of a bad one to make a good one, but to make a good one better, or out of many good ones, one principal good one" (quoted in Bobrick, 2001, p. 249).[25] By this point in history, the assembled scholars had become aware of an entire literature in other languages, such as Chaldee (Aramaic), Syrian, Spanish, and Dutch (Bobrick, 2001, pp. 238 & 249; Greenslade, 1963, p. 166). Accordingly, there was work to do for dozens of men, divided into six "companies."[26] Then, they had to reconcile and interweave their various contributions to achieve a sufficient continuity of tone throughout.

---

[24] The king grew to regret it. Bobrick reports that in his last speech to parliament, Henry VIII literally wept that Holy Writ was "disputed, rhymed, sung and jangled in every ale-house and tavern" (2001, p. 160).

[25] Roland Frye (1965) commented, "No committee has ever by itself created a great work of art. What they did was to perfect a great work of art" (1965, p. xxxiv).

[26] The identities and titles of these men are known (Bobrick, 2001, appendix 4; Norton, 2011, ch. 3).

Undoubtedly, leadership occurred during these scholarly disputations, not least by Richard Bancroft; but the obvious thing should not go unsaid: namely, that there was no single individual to be credited with the translation. The KJV was far less of a solitary effort than Martin Luther's had been over in Saxony (Harter, 2017). As Bobrick pointed out, "[i]ndividual genius was not, perhaps, what was called for" (2001, p. 259).[27] The influx of new knowledge and parallel efforts in other languages to translate the original from across Europe amplifies the fact that this was truly a collaborative effort arising out of the times in which they lived.

After issuing their 1611 first edition to little fanfare, the companies that wrote it disbanded. Nevertheless, scholars kept trying to tweak it for decades, so that if you were to refer to the King James Bible, someone might ask which one you meant (Norton, 2011, ch. 6). It took many years and many attempts to revise. Ultimately, the KJV did become preeminent for centuries, so that today we might call it "the authentic, elderly, increasingly disregarded but still revered monarch among Bibles" (Norton, 2011, p. 180). A complete history of any translation into the vernacular would include its subsequent reception and significance down through the ages – factors that draw things further and further away from the exertions of any single individual and distribute agency far and wide. This phase of the story is more plainly sociological than anything we might refer to as leadership studies. McGrath even admits that the triumph of the KJV, many years later, had little to do with the merits of the translation itself and more to do with the restoration of the monarchy in 1660 (2001, p. 289; see Norton, 2011, p. 138). So, once again, not unsurprisingly politics intrudes.[28] Yet, even in the telling of the story, there had been influential figures such as James I, Wycliffe, and Tyndale (and Bancroft) whose individual exertions shaped the final product. Leadership certainly occurred, yet the more significant finding is that the KJV was the product of a dedicated team of scholars imbued

---

[27] David Norton reprinted in full the translator's preface to the reader and then remarked sardonically that given how awkwardly it reads, maybe we should be glad that this bunch hadn't tried to write the translation themselves (2011, p. 113).

[28] In a bizarre twist, the English language Bible that initially upheld the monarchy eventually inspired a revolution against the monarchy (Bobrick, 2001, p. 12; Bragg, 2011, ch. 7). Later, the Civil Rights leadership in the United States did much the same thing. Bragg wrote: "They took the words of their enemy and used them to fight and ultimately overcome them" (2011, p. 97, also chs. 18 & 19). Melvyn Bragg (2011), a novelist susceptible to extravagant claims, described what was being done in the name of the KJV at the time of the Glorious Revolution (1642–1651): "Men called themselves 'Saints.' Communism was advocated and practiced, as was free love, the preaching by women and the virtue of nakedness. Innocents were murdered, property was razed, all institutions were interrogated (p. 82)." Eventually, Bragg credits the KJV with shaping the English language, English and American literature, politics (including both democracy and socialism), culture, religion, education, early modern science, the slave trade, feminism, and temperance, as well as inciting opposition such as the Enlightenment.

with a rising interest in the languages of antiquity that was taking place across Europe at the same time.

Translating the Bible from Latin into English had been the project of several pioneers, but the KJV was an exemplary collaboration. And as Frye noted, the English Renaissance was uniquely suited for the task (1965, p. xxix), even if its literary luminaries such as Shakespeare did not take part. Bragg quoted Samuel Johnson to the effect that here was a golden age and the beginning of literary perfection (2011, p. 140), a special time.[29] The final product might have taken a while to gain widespread acceptance, but once it did, the KJV shaped religion, politics, and literature throughout the British empire for generations to come.

4.4 Concluding Thoughts

In the study of cultural dynamics, Ortega y Gasset advised using the generation as a unit of measure. To be sure, at any given point in time, individuals struggle against one another to preserve, question, and displace elements of the prevailing culture as it was handed down to them from prior generations. Speaking broadly, the culture itself flows relatively unchanged, with only pockets of reform. Yet, the historically significant transformations require collective, coordinated action. Such a transformation often begins as resistance to some feature in the prevailing culture, with various participants casting about for suitable alternatives. Some alternatives work better than others. When enough of these critics begin to collaborate and coalesce around a distinctive response to the culture, one sees the potential for a more thoroughgoing transformation.

Antonio Gramsci, often regarded as a cultural Marxist, attended to these dynamics with care, inasmuch as he concurred that culture is passed along from one generation to the next. If one were to alter a given culture, therefore, the best place to intervene – the fulcrum, as it were – would be during the transmission of that culture. Change what is taught, and you change the culture. How then does one change what is being taught? That project begins

---

[29] The Elizabethan Age is widely known to be a time of renaissance and literary acclaim. Nevertheless, the Elizabethan Age as it pertains to literature extends into the reign of James I. According to H. Frank Heath, "[a] great deal of the most characteristic Elizabethan literature was written in the reign of James ... It is a commonplace to say ... that its literature is the greatest our country has produced" (1991, p. 1 f.). George Saintsbury had made an equivalent assertion in *A History of Elizabethan Literature*, where he claimed that the lauded age reached its maturity during the reign of James (1902, p. 454). For it was a unique moment, a confluence of many things: a Renaissance interest across Europe in classical languages (centered in universities); a Reformation zeal to propagate scripture in the vernacular (centered in Protestant circles); an increasing use of the printing press; a dawning awareness of the beauty of the English language, just as English arms and trade emerged as globally dominant; and a monarch keen to see the project done for largely political reasons.

by influencing the educators. But a culture is transmitted as much by other means, such as the arts, journalism, and entertainment, that together they constitute what he called hegemony. That is, cultural institutions tend to reinforce one another, telling the same basic story. A radical transformation, therefore, will concentrate on transforming these cultural institutions first. Politics, law, and economics would inevitably follow. Such a massive undertaking requires a generation.

Gramsci himself did not succeed in transforming the world directly. After a season as head of the Communist Party in Italy, he was imprisoned by authorities, fell quite ill, and died before convalescence. The world at that time was at war, his political party was outlawed, and Mussolini governed Italy. It took ten years to publish his *Prison Notebooks* (subsequently translated and compiled by the Columbia University Press in 2011). And it was not until the 1980s that his stature as an intellectual was finally secured. Subsequently, however, his views on cultural dynamics have influenced a diverse range of academic disciplines, as well as social actors who shared his vision. In short, he was a theorist in search of a generation sufficient to implement that vision. Subsequently, it took lesser intellectuals such as Herbert Marcuse and Saul Alinsky to translate Gramsci's teachings into a more practical course of action. Their success is a matter of dispute, of course, but one can readily see their shared embrace of the doctrine that the unit of analysis for cultural shifts of any consequence is the generation. Thought leaders are not enough.

5 Cultural Elaboration on Issues of Race

Margaret Archer contends that cultural dynamics can be understood as a struggle with contradictions and compatibilities. Contradictions set two sides against one another, during which one side or the other prevails, or the two sides compromise, or they are transcended completely by some third possibility. Leadership during these ongoing episodes can manifest as partisans, mediators, and those who see a way to transcend the contradiction altogether. Compatibilities, on the other hand, tend to reinforce one another like positive feedback loops, extending and intensifying a sense of coherence that can lapse into groupthink and intolerance. Both occur at the same time in any society. This section takes as its historical example the contradiction of ostensibly Christian regimes adopting policies based upon race such as slavery and apartheid. One can witness what Archer labeled social morphogenesis in the career of William F. Buckley, Jr., who struggled to recognize and overcome the contradiction in American conservatism with regard to race.

5.1 Introduction

The twenty-first century continues to witness civic unrest on the basis of race. Racial conflict of one kind or another seems to have existed before the dawn of civilization and emerges repeatedly around the world. Psychologists even suspect that the tendency to sort humanity into Us versus Them, friend or foe, is intrinsic. Our powers of differentiation guide human beings toward that which is safe and wholesome and away from that which is not. Our evolutionary success probably depended on some version of those powers to discriminate who can be trusted. Its manifestation in modernity, however, ranging from slavery and apartheid to genocide, has elicited outrage and revulsion. Indeed, race as a basis for distinguishing among human beings socially has been increasingly rejected.

The preceding section introduced the idea of the generation as the appropriate unit of analysis when it comes to cultural dynamics. The purpose of this section is to illustrate the relationship of culture and leadership by exposing an egregious example of a cultural contradiction that leaders can use (or misuse) to bring about cultural change. In other words, here we will take a closer look at causal mechanisms. To be candid, in this particular context, the transformation comes slowly; the work is not yet done. But we have a record of leadership that exemplifies and points to the possibility of change. Before getting to the specific example, however, this section will rely on Margaret Archer's efforts to explain these causal mechanisms known as social morphogenesis.[30]

5.2 Some Elements of the Cultural System Are Contradictory, Some Are Compatible

A cultural system will contain elements that contradict one another and elements that reinforce one another. Each possibility can influence participants in how they choose to behave. A contradiction will raise the possibility of pressure on participants to resolve it. Compatible elements, like positive feedback loops, will reassure participants and give them greater confidence to act, often to the point that they ignore contrary evidence or other possibilities.

5.2.1 Contradictions/Conflict

Any cultural system includes an inexhaustible number of apparent contradictions, most of which participants ignore or regard as inconsequential, to the extent they are even aware of them (Archer, 1996, p. 146; see Voegelin, 1956,

---

[30] Archer's argument mirrors the sociological theory of Gabriel de Tarde in *The Laws of Imitation* (1895/1903).

pp. 45–47). That is to say, people may evade the situational logic (1996, p. 158). A Christian people adopting a liberal polity would have a tough time rationalizing the fact that it once tolerated the institution of slavery. Yet, it happened. Any given culture undergoes internal conflict of some sort (Moody-Adams, 1997, p. 31). Occasionally, a contradiction does influence behavior of one kind or another, and even though what an individual person will do in response to that contradiction will vary, we can refer to the role of culture in those instances as *cultural conditioning* (Archer, 1996, p. 144).

One of the most poignant examples was portrayed in the novel *The Adventures of Huckleberry Finn* by Mark Twain (1885), when a young white boy is rafting along the Mississippi River with his friend, the slave known as Jim. Huck considered Jim a friend, but he also recognized that by floating away, he was helping Jim to escape. Should he turn his friend over to the authorities? Huck's dilemma, set forth in Jonathan Bennett's famous article "The Conscience of Huckleberry Finn" (1974), highlights the discrepancy that people were once expected to live with.

In its simplest form, we can designate the contradiction as an incompatibility between the two positions A and B. (Obviously, the reality is far more complicated.) When a participant chooses to do something about the contradiction, they can alter or discard A, alter or discard B, or alter them both in order to bring about a degree of consistency, which Archer called *syncretism* (1996, pp. 158 f. & 171). At the sociocultural level, where participants interact, there are likely to be partisans for A and partisans for B, so that the process of resolving an apparent contradiction in the culture will take the form of a struggle, whether by that we mean debates, elections, or outright civil war. But that overt part – the outward manifestation – comes later. At the conditioning stage, before the analysis of how people interact, where it is a matter of situational logic, an individual participant like Huck Finn is confronted with a decision about A and B. He runs smack into the contradiction.

What are the behavioral implications of believing that A is true and B represents a contradiction? Let us suppose, said Archer, that partisans of A must account for B somehow. It is not going away. You can neither embrace B altogether when you are a partisan of A, nor can you reject B out of hand (1996, p. 154 f.). You are a Christian who must somehow reconcile the tenets of your religion with the brutal practice of slavery. As Archer put it, "the inconsistency has to be tackled, repaired and the correction made to stick" (1996, p. 157). How is that done? Partisans for A will likely turn first to modifying B to fit A, so that regardless of the outcome, A will survive. Likewise, in a mirror image, a partisan for B will hope to modify A. Out of this process of mutual modification, B might come to be replaced with a more congenial version, B_1. In this fashion, the contradiction just might collapse without further controversy. But then if B_1 (or A_1) fails to bring about a reconciliation, partisans can reach for B_2 or A_2, and so forth, hoping to get the other side to bend. In many instances, this works. Slaveholders often resorted to pointing out the examples in the Christian Bible of slavery and slaveholding, as though a Christian *opposition* to the institution of slavery was unscriptural. They were hoping at the very least to turn A_1 (abolition) into A_2 (grudging toleration).

Sometimes, A can be retained at the expense of B altogether, or B can be retained at the expense of A. But when this does not work, the partisans might be persuaded to compromise, each of them modifying their position until they can be made to reconcile by a process of mutual adjustment. This step implies a third possibility. After trying to alter B to become B_1 or altering both A and B to become A_1 and B_1, respectively, on some occasions, a partisan of A might be forced to reexamine A without demanding that B undergo any alteration whatsoever. That is, one might move from A to A_1 on their own initiative, as a way of preserving something of A while conceding the viability of B. A slaveholder might modify his or her views, for instance, resolving to release their slaves upon their death or maybe accepting slavery as a necessary evil, to be eradicated in due time, but not yet. In other words: "if I cannot get you to alter your position and we cannot each alter our respective positions, in some instances maybe I should consider altering my own position unilaterally." Archer identifies three outcomes when the partisan of A reconsiders the merits of A: accommodation with B, degeneration of A (to A_1), and the extinction of A (1996, p. 169).

Over time, these various adjustments can strengthen the cultural system as a whole and improve both A and B. But they can also degrade A or B to the point where either becomes a pale semblance of the original – or in the words of D. G. Ritchie, "grown tame and sleek" (quoted in Moody-Adams, 1997, p. 59). Once you revise A and no longer insist on keeping it pure, it becomes increasingly easier to revise it further, until the motivation on behalf of the remnants of A dwindles to nothing (Archer, 1996, p. 171). Things might get watered down so much that they lose their power, becoming ghosts of their former selves or objects of derision. It is not beyond the realm of possibility that A or B could vanish altogether. In the twenty-first century, to cite an obvious example, most Christians find it incomprehensible that their forebearers ever tolerated enslaving other people.

Thomas Kuhn (2012) famously studied this process during episodes of scientific revolutions, as for example, when the geocentric model of the solar system kept making tactical retreats under the increasing plausibility of the heliocentric model. The rearguard actions by partisans of the geocentric model became almost outlandish before the struggle was finally resolved in favor of the heliocentric model. A became A_1 and then A_2 and A_3, and so forth, until it was extinguished.

Christians today forget that after abolition, their forebearers retained many of the same practices and attitudes for more than a hundred years. Jim Crow, for example (A_1), may have been a tepid version of racism (A) compared to slavery, but it was a residue all the same. Thus, this is not to suggest that the process always ends with a clear winner and a clear loser. Like I said, some compromises will survive. A_1 and B_1 might both be made weaker as a result, or they might become more palatable (or at least less egregious). In such a manner, historians often witness the evolution of a culture.

We should also recognize that in many instances, the resolution of an apparent contradiction between A and B turns out to be their replacement by C – that is, a fresh position that retains little or nothing of either A or B. Consequently, the contradiction evaporates. For instance, the debate over a Christian position with regard to slavery disappears when you no longer recognize Christianity's authority, one way or the other. Of course, the process by which C displaces A and B will resemble the struggle between A and B, only at a higher level of abstraction. In principle, according to Archer, this process of surfacing and dealing with contradictions can continue indefinitely. Every resolution is provisional (1996, p. 161). Dying creeds can go underground or be resurrected. History is replete with examples. There is no reason to believe it will ever end.

We now have the permutations in their simplest form: what survives would be some version of A only, some version of B only, versions of both A and B together, and neither A nor B in any version.

Contradiction does not determine what individual participants will do. They are still free to choose. But the awareness of a contradiction could spur participants to do something or constrain them from a course of action that they would otherwise have taken, so that the culture shapes what people do. We should not be surprised when leadership emerges during these struggles, on behalf of one side or the other (either A or B), or on behalf of the spirit of reconciliation (both A and B). Many of the most celebrated leaders, however, championed a position C that made both A and B simply irrelevant. Each "side" has its leaders: partisans, mediators, and those who transcend the entire squabble.

5.2.2 Compatibility/Complementarity

Compatibility also shapes behavior by means of cultural conditioning. In this instance, B appears to be compatible with A. Again, most participants will not even notice or care, yet there will be occasions when the compatibility has an impact. The presence of B is likely to reinforce A and convince participants that

A and B are mutually correct. Participants will step out with greater confidence. They will also tend to ignore evidence to the contrary and dismiss voices of dissent. In fact, because A reinforces B and B reinforces A, it is thought that a person would have to be perverse not to accede.

I quote Archer directly:

> [T]he adherents of A are enmeshed in the cluster forming the concomitant compatibility and insulated against those outside it. Yet because their 'truths' are not challenged but only reinforced from the proximate environment, then actors confront no ideational problems, are propelled to no daring feats of intellectual elaboration, but work according to a situational logic which stimulates nothing beyond cultural embroidery. The net effect of this is to reduce Systemic diversity to variations on a theme (which do however increase its density) and to intensify Socio-Cultural uniformity (through the absence of alternatives). (1996, p. 158)

What Archer is describing is a large-scale version of groupthink. The worst result is stultification, stasis, and a temptation toward intolerance of anything contrary.

To be fair, it takes time and intention to build and protect any system of belief. These things do not happen overnight of their own accord (Archer, 1996, p. 172 f; see generally James, 1907; Meek, 2014; Quine & Ullian, 1978). Speaking broadly, people want their culture to be an integrated whole, believing that "God's in his heaven – all's right with the world." A culture must feel so natural that you barely notice it. The experience of compatibility between A and B first generates curiosity and gratification, as it affirms what people knew. Archer called it a period of euphoria (1996, p. 174). Soon, people will look for adjacent problems and see whether they too are susceptible to the same treatment. If it works for both A and B, maybe it also works for C.[31] With every discovery, as the web of beliefs became increasingly extensive and inclusive, more people found it attractive. Not only does the web grow outward, it also becomes denser and more intricate as it consolidates into a *consensus* (Archer, 1996, p. 175 f.). In the process, the emerging consensus turns to the task of boundary formation and boundary maintenance (p. 177 f.). That is to say that an interest in purity tends to differentiate that which affirms the consensus from what does not, as charges of heresy erupt, and "true believers" slowly gain power. In a further step, then, adherents of the consensus seek to reproduce by means of propaganda, education, and in some cases coercion, so that the entire

---

[31] Archer used the example of Utilitarianism. The rudiments of Utilitarianism were found to help explain economics, public policy, law, ethics, and to a lesser extent the natural sciences (1996, p. 175). The more things it could explain, the more entrenched it came to be as part of the culture.

web displaces rival accounts (Archer, 1996, pp. 178–183). The culture under-standably raises partisans of the consensus, defenders of the status quo.

Something of the sort occurred in the United States, in the Antebellum South, where an entire latticework of institutions tended to mesh, constituting a distinct identity that led the confederacy to imagine that it could flourish as a separate nation-state, with its own peculiar institution and what they regarded as a cherished way of life.

5.2.3 Both Conflict and Compatibility

The truth is that no cultural system ultimately succeeds in driving out its rivals, for even at its zenith, the consensus conceals inconsistencies and discrepancies that will persist and give critics an opportunity to challenge the status quo. Defenders of the consensus will try to sustain it in part by ignoring or actively suppressing alternatives. Tactics include censorship, exile, and incarceration (Archer, 1996, p. 190 f.). Another tactic is to urge dissenters to go live elsewhere (p. 196 f.). Beyond a certain point, however, authoritarian tactics will not work (pp. 191–197). Because it was a fiction to begin with, purity is unsustainable. Gradually, almost imperceptibly, individuals who uncover these hidden contra-dictions will desert the consensus. Maybe they will identify one another and recognize what we might call a countercompatibility, creating a sect that is satisfied to live apart. But as we just saw, the time may come when the sect abandons its separate existence and instead rises up to displace the prevailing consensus (pp. 198–203). When that starts to happen, defenders of the status quo tell themselves that they were right about the threat that they were trying to suppress: "I told you they were up to no good."

Culture is comprised of many such conflicts at different stages of develop-ment. Not only are there vestiges of a former consensus still hanging around, but a number of different alternatives struggle against one another while trying to displace the dominant consensus. Martin Luther King, Jr. preached one approach to race relations, but Malcolm X preached another. And while one sector of the culture might have reached one stage in the process (the US military was formally integrated in 1948), another sector might have reached a different stage (Black Lives Matter continues to exist after 2020 to draw attention to disparate treatment by law enforcement). Cultural dynamics never stop. Antonio Gramsci had argued that Karl Marx was wrong to seek revolution by means of politics; better instead to work through cultural institutions such as the media, the arts, and education (see Landy, 1986). The entire culture does not turn all at the same time in the same direction in concert. Thus, culture is always ripe for leadership.

5.3 Issues of Race in the Civic Order

Carl Schmitt once argued that the defining distinction in all politics is between friend and enemy. He wrote that nations continue to define themselves in this way and that an ensuing conflict always remains a possibility (1976, p. 28). Even Christians who preach love above all else have repeatedly fought unbelievers when they were not fighting one another (1976, p. 29). Schmitt claimed that everything political has meaning only as it pertains to this age-old compulsion to identify and contend with the Other, whoever that Other happens to be. Domains such as economics, religion, and even art can be recruited to conduct political conflict. Nevertheless, politics as the search for civic order is a separate undertaking. He added that any other associations, leagues, partnerships, and affiliations will be pushed aside once the political emerges; during wartime, your coworker or mentor or colleague from the other side becomes hateful (1976, p. 38). If anything, the political has taken on the absolute conviction and fervor that used to be attributed only to religion. And in Schmitt's opinion, that is just as well (1976, p. 65). It is more honest, he said. Schmitt admitted that plenty of people in any community might be optimistic and prefer to disavow this basic fact, but despite their best efforts, all it takes is just a spark, some fresh outrage, for the enmity to flare up (1976, p. 66). He added that these optimists who claim not to think in such stark, binary terms will have formed the same division between themselves and those who threaten the peace, so that even when they cry "peace," they engage in behavior compatible with conflict. Our human tendency for binaries feeds into animosity.

It is not my purpose to accept Schmitt's assertions. It is enough to acknowledge that it exists as a justification for making pernicious distinctions. It is at least a rationalization for a phenomenon that keeps recurring. The leadership scholar Howard Gardner (2006) posited that this tendency is an ineradicable feature of the human psyche, discernible even in infants. The popular memes about children having to be taught to hate are empirically incorrect – a lesson dramatized by William Golding in *Lord of the Flies* (1954). Perhaps the most famous theorist concerning this topic was Konrad Lorenz, whose 1966 translation referred to the biological programming to aggress (Lorenz, 1966). His findings are not without controversy, but at least we should allude to this literature and have it accessible when discussing the problematic issue of race in politics. Lamentably, we might be hardwired for bias.

As background on trying to understand how people identify the Other (with a capital "O"), one must accept that the very idea of race has a troubled history in the scientific community, such that biologically speaking it will be difficult to draw clear boundaries. Some scholars have given up and declared that race is a social construct and not a biological category of any utility. This has not prevented race from being a political factor to this day.

The emergence of slavery, apartheid, and the Shoah were in turn preceded by widespread prejudice, such that these institutions did not emerge *ex nihilo*. They were if anything formalizations and intensifications of an existing animus. The fact that their authors also espoused Christian values demonstrates the principle that Archer had described of a perceived compatibility within the culture. Only much later did the incongruity actually "condition" effective leadership in response. For representative leaders who used these discrepancies to assert themselves, one thinks, for example, of Martin Luther King, Jr., Desmond Tutu, and Dietrich Bonhoeffer – clergymen all.

Race as a social construct relies on the perception of differences, as a way of classifying or categorizing people. Racism as an ideology adds a further dimension about the relative value or worth of these differences. For many, race has been understood "to establish the limits of possibilities" (Heilke, 1990, p. 61). Different races were deemed to be good at different things, but in the competition for value or worth, racism presupposes that at least on average one race will outperform another and bears greater worth.[32] To be blunt, one race is presumed to be not as smart, in the same way that children, domesticated animals, and mental defectives are not as capable with regard to the higher faculties such as reason. Dominance was to be based on a natural superiority, a position stated bluntly by Aristotle. Needless to say, the emergence of demonstrably superior members of the dominated race such as Frederick Douglas already created an empirical problem with these presuppositions. If we are superior, they ask, then why is he so much smarter, articulate, and influential? Counterexamples pose problems to the consensus.[33]

Another problem with a racist worldview is presupposing that biological differences determine mental and spiritual capacities, as if to say that one inherits these capacities (Heilke, 1990, pp. 80 & 108). Even the natural sciences leading up to World War II had rejected this claim: "Intellectual and spiritual traits are not directly accessible to the natural sciences, nor can they be simply

---

[32] In some instances, the reverse is true. The dominant class fears that they are not in fact superior. In a letter dated 1963 (published in 2007, pp. 461–464), Eric Voegelin recounted that prior to the Anschluss (the forcible union of Germany and Austria in 1938), a group of colleagues on the faculty where he worked in Austria told people that Voegelin was a Jew (which he was not). When Voegelin asked the ringleader why he had done so, the man confessed, "Our people aren't as clever as you!"

[33] I chose the term "articulate" for two reasons. For one thing, Douglas admirably fit the definition of the term. For another, the term was often used by white folks to connote a black person who spoke surprisingly (and uncharacteristically) clearly, at least as eruditely as they did. Thus, it had acquired a condescending utility, not unlike saying that a child is precocious (see Alim & Smitherman, 2012; Rini, 2020).

associated with faculties localizable in genetic material" (Heilke, 1990, p. 110). There was even considerable evidence at the time that race was an inadequate way to categorize people *biologically*! This fact obviously did not stop communities from using race to make civic distinctions – a fact that cast doubt once again upon regimes supposedly grounded in the natural sciences. "Follow the science," they would say, but the science was against them.

One could extend the critique further to point out that a civic order is united by intangible things and not race. It was a very old belief in Western thought that the community is centered around an idea (a faith or creed or image) and not the laws of descent (Heilke, 1990, p. 122). The belief that communities defined themselves exclusively through lineage had been challenged repeatedly, especially in cultures that belonged to the Christian episteme. One can go back to antiquity, where the usual methods of passing authority from one generation to the next was determined in Israel not by heredity, as one might suppose, but by some kind of anointing (Voegelin, 1956). Often, divine favor bypassed the descendants of a patriarch or judge, and when the people asked YHWH to establish a system with a royal family in Israel, the first choice (Saul) proved to be unworthy and had to be removed, and subsequent heirs to the throne exhibited an uneven record, such that divine unction transferred instead to the prophets. The argument that the civic order was to be based exclusively on consanguinity had not been incontestably true in the West for centuries.[34]

Furthermore, race-based policies distort the sociological phenomenon of an elite from out of which leaders arise by fixing in advance based on genetics who will be qualified to lead, which misperceives the nature of leadership itself as a relationship of mutual accord for shared purpose.[35] At best, a racial distinction undergirds not so much leadership as domination, which is why we might question whether slavery even qualifies as leadership regarding the victims. Does the master in any sense "lead" the servant? It is not my purpose to argue that these practices were enactments of leadership. In fact, I deny that they were. But, what I am trying to say is that the relationship between the races influenced the culture that prevailed within the dominant race, where in fact leadership was routinely practiced.

The ruling class in many slave-holding countries were ostensibly Christian (see generally Bradley et al., 2011–2017). The American South is still considered to belong to what is known pejoratively as the Bible Belt. The Boers in South Africa were influenced by the descendants of Huguenot refugees, but

---

[34] Obviously, Europe had gone through an extended era in which royalty and other properties did pass to the eldest legitimate male heir by means of primogeniture, but even then their power and status was to be subordinated to the Church and to God.

[35] See e.g. DuBois, 1903, quoted in Wren, 1995, ch. 17.

ultimately subscribed to the Dutch Reformed Church, while at the same time instituting apartheid. The British, who won the Boer War and contributed to the imposition of apartheid, were formally Anglican. Accepting Christianity as the grounds of civic authority raises many discrepancies about its teachings that contradict racist policies.

Jesus in his ministry did not restrict his mission to the Jews but reached to outsiders such as the Canaanite woman (*Matthew* 15:21–28) and taught his disciples to avoid these pernicious distinctions. His domain was not biologically determined. For all have sinned and fallen short of the glory of God (*Romans* 3:23–24). Instead, he preached a kingdom of the spirit. The church that emerged after his resurrection had to address this problem of racial distinctions beginning with the phenomenon of Pentecost in which the Good News was preached to all, regardless of race (*Acts of the Apostles* 2). Philip subsequently delivered the message to an Ethiopian (*Acts* 8:26–40). Peter had to be convinced in a vision to proselytize to a Roman centurion and his pagan household. He said

> You are well aware that it is against our law for a Jew to associate with or visit a Gentile. But God has shown me that I should not call anyone impure or unclean. So when I was sent for, I came without raising any objection.
>
> (*Acts* 10:28–29)

Paul convinced the Apostles to spread the word to the heathen throughout Asia Minor. Paul even wrote specifically: "There is neither Jew nor Gentile, neither slave nor free, nor is there male and female, for you are all one in Christ Jesus" (*Galatians* 3:28).

For these and many further reasons, the culture that conditioned leadership during eras of racist policy contained many logical and empirical incompatibilities. Christianity just could not support the prevailing public policy. Nevertheless, these cultural institutions did occur. They were justified in part by specious compatibilities. For example, that God had given them a new dispensation, replacing the New Testament. Or that the claims for dignity under God apply only to those who are sufficiently rational/educated. Many slave-owners regarded their slaves as little more than children who are actually better off enslaved, such that it was a ministry to control them. Or they had to import them to North America in order to convert them to Christianity. Or apologists cited scripture supporting the institution of slavery, as it existed in biblical times. The Boers and British justified apartheid as an arrangement among multiple tribes, like a confederation. So they denied that their motivation was based on race per se. Instead, it was based on the volatile political mixture among the diverse and quarreling African peoples. In other words, defenders of the status quo accumulated arguments that mutually reinforce one another.

Then, because of confirmation bias, they could point to the evidence and say, "look, our superiority has been demonstrated by our dominance." Or, they (the purportedly inferior peoples) are demonstrably less capable as proven by test scores or the paucity of their "kind" in positions of responsibility, which really is a circular argument. But then, that is the point: the mutually reinforcing arguments prop one another up and thereby justify the whole.

Plenty of participants deserted these oppressive cultures, in one form or another, but leadership manifested in the fostering of dissent. Often, clubs or groups such as the Abolitionists formed to resist. That resistance took many forms, ranging from electoral politics to outright rebellion. Resistance was often couched in terms of the contradiction described by Archer. Consequently, leadership arose on every side, even if it took far too long to manifest.

5.4 The March for Civil Rights

Many leadership scholars invoke the memory of Martin Luther King, Jr. as exemplary of leadership. Few have tied his efforts to causal mechanisms, such as those described by Margaret Archer; instead, they tend to portray MLK (as he is known) as a solitary champion on behalf of his people confronting a vast and monolithic (and malevolent) social system. That romantic interpretation of his ministry misconstrues the cultural dynamics. Even in his own words, MLK identified a contradiction in the culture between A and B. It was never his goal to supplant the prevailing culture or withdraw his followers into insular enclaves in order to live according to a different culture. He sought to uphold the shared culture best by eradicating the persistent contradiction. Here was a man imbued by a culture, educated highly and nurtured, a product of that culture, a man who wanted that culture to live up to its own ideals.

At the risk of grossly oversimplifying MLK's mission, he drew attention to a contradiction between A and B, and urged society to see it starkly and fix it once and for all by choosing A as opposed to B. Although a representative of B did finally silence the clergyman in Memphis, Tennessee on April 4, 1968, the assassination was not before MLK's indictment of the culture had resounded. The man had posed a question and refused to let that question be ignored: namely, would the United States at long last disavow the incompatible doctrines of race and extend its franchise fully to the Negro?

Even though the contradiction first appeared on the shores of the New World in the 1600s (see *New York Times Magazine*, 2019), it was a long time in becoming part of the cultural landscape. *Uncle Tom's Cabin* shone a light on it in 1852. Abraham Lincoln had understood the contradiction a hundred years before MLK ("Letter to Joshua Speed, 24 August 1855," in Lincoln, 1953–

1955). It is not as though MLK was the first person to notice the contradiction. Nevertheless, he was urging his fellow Americans to resolve it. He was not so much opposed to the individual racists as to their abiding contradiction. For he believed that for them to quit their racism would bless them, too, and not just the African Americans organized against them. Resolution of the contradiction would contribute to the integrity of the whole.

It is also significant for our purposes that MLK was not interested solely in governmental structures – that is, in laws and policies – for much of that work had already been done, going all the way back to the Declaration of Independence, the Emancipation Proclamation, and various amendments to the Constitution of the United States. The structures compatible with America's ideals as to equality were in place. MLK's grievance was with their perversion and neglect. His struggle was less about politics and more about culture.

Evidence exists that his efforts made a difference. Evidence also exists that his dream has not been realized yet in its entirety. The cultural contradiction itself persists, as protests in 2020 over the slaying of George Floyd remind us. Nevertheless, MLK illustrates a leader's participation in the causal mechanisms set forth by Margaret Archer. Neither of them – Archer nor MLK – was so naïve as to think that culture would completely purify itself of contradictions forever. Nevertheless, leadership did occur, and the culture is shifting perceptibly, as the following example illustrates.

5.5 The Morphogenesis of William F. Buckley, Jr.

> Sometimes . . . cultures are perpetuated by human beings who are uncritically committed to the continuance of a way of life.
>
> (Moody-Adams, 1997, p. 101)

A young Bill Buckley had assembled a motley of conservatives in 1955 to launch a journal whose stated purpose was "to stand athwart history, yelling Stop." At the time, he was trying to accommodate anticommunists, traditional Catholics, law-and-order types, free market enthusiasts, and not a few cranks with nowhere else to publish their opposition to the prevailing creeds of postwar America. Buckley himself was a peculiar blend of South Carolinan aristocracy and Texas horse sense,[36] a young man who found himself tirelessly commenting on issues of the day, including the Civil Rights movement. Not unnaturally, given his upbringing, he favored segregation and resisted the entreaties of the black community. In 1957, he wrote an infamous editorial on "Why the South

---

[36] For biographical details, see e.g. Bogus (2011), Buckley & Buckley (1979), and Judis (1988).

Must Prevail." His journal *National Review* continues to be cited from that era to prove that WFB (as he is known) was a racist.

Recently, Alvin Felzenberg accumulated the evidence for this proposition in a 2017 article in *Politico* (Felzenberg, 2017), where he concluded that cultural elaboration took place in the heart and mind of this popular polemicist. At one time, WFB was indeed a defender of the status quo in the Jim Crow states, but the cultural contradiction of that position became increasingly intolerable to him personally. Felzenberg cites several influences.

First, WFB had been emerging in the conservative movement as something of an arbiter of what was and what was not acceptable as conservatism; he would eventually declare (for example) that the John Birch Society, Ayn Rand, and anti-Semitism had no place in the movement. Over time, he felt responsibility for addressing the incompatibilities in what it even means to be a conservative (see generally Buckley & Kesler, 1988). Ultimately, he had to consider the possibility that racism too did not fit.

Second, WFB was a devout Roman Catholic who started to recognize the incompatibility of the Christian ethos with race politics. In 1963, he asked his mother plaintively how she reconciled her faith with her acceptance of race codes. He was quite aware of the animus against Catholics in his own lifetime, so he was able to transfer his equivalent grievances to the African American community. Maybe his original position against them was not unlike the position that many had taken against Catholics. It certainly impressed him that the Civil Rights movement was intertwined in its mission with black churches.[37]

Third, as a journalist, he actually visited predominately black cities in 1969 after a series of race riots, in order to speak with their leaders and look at living conditions in what was known as the ghetto. During this tour, sponsored by the Urban League, it became evident that whereas left-leaning journalists curried favor with these spokesmen, already disposed to agree with what they were hearing, WFB asked hard questions and showed a genuine willingness to take the content of their claims seriously. He earned grudging respect because he was actually *listening* to them (see Buckley, 1970, pp. 153–166).

Fourth, at a time when various minority activists and critics had trouble finding airtime to explain their grievances on the only three television networks, WFB would invite them as guests to his long-running television show "Firing Line" – where he certainly debated them about their views, but at least he gave them a forum in which to express those views (Hendershot, 2016; see generally

---

[37] For an account of his religious perspective, see generally Buckley (1997).

Buckley, 1989). The show featured such luminaries as James Baldwin, Muhammed Ali, Eldridge Cleaver, Jesse Jackson, Huey Newton, Cornel West, Eleanor Holmes Norton, Julian Bond, and John Lewis.[38] This opportunity gave them a forum. And they in turn gave WFB an education.

To be fair, WFB's motivation was mixed. He seemed to be reacting as much against the populist white politicians such as George Wallace who repulsed him and whose antics prompted federal intervention, which WFB regarded as an unconstitutional assertion of power. He regarded such political bedfellows with repugnance. WFB literally wept when covering a 1963 bombing in Birmingham that killed four little girls. Furthermore, as a champion of "law-and-order" he may have wanted to suppress black violence, sometimes brutally, but he also had to acknowledge lawless tactics by bigoted southerners to deny African Americans the vote. You can't stick up for law-and-order, he realized, and then condone these extralegal abridgments. "Major, deep reforms are necessary," wrote WFB on June 3 of that year (1970, p. 160 f.).

One can see in the example of this pundit – a widely known representative of conservative, Republican, white, southern, traditional, capitalist sensibilities from twentieth-century America – the cultural dynamics of elaboration analyzed in abstract terms by Margaret Archer. Nicholas Buccola (2019) judges WFB's responses as too little, too late, but then he clearly recognizes the struggle that had been going on in WFB's heart (see e.g. 2019, p. 363). Nevertheless, Buccola rejects WFB's many public disavowals of violence against the black community as more of a revulsion against violence per se, rather than an enlightened position on civil rights. The point is that WFB occupied a liminal space where cultural elaboration was taking place during a time of upheaval. The fact that Buccola fails to recognize the possibility of cultural change (and insists that conservatism as an ideology is still – and always will be – inherently racist) says more about his static perspective. The truth is otherwise.

> One principal aim of the non-violent protests of the civil rights movement, in [Rev.] King's words, was precisely to create a "crisis," or a "tension in the mind," whereby supporters of segregation would be forced to confront the social reality of segregation. But the point of creating this tension was to produce circumstances in which at least some segregationists would eventually be rationally compelled to admit the inconsistency between democratic principles of equality and legally sanctioned discrimination on the basis of race. (Moody-Adams, 1997, p. 199, omitting citations and italics)

---

[38] For an unapologetically biased account of WFB's debate with James Baldwin, see Buccola (2019).

6 Closing

When it comes to studying leadership, culture matters. Yet, a theoretical definition of the term "culture" has been elusive, if not impossible. The idea of
culture seems to incorporate an array of many loosely integrated things.
Nevertheless, it has been possible to frame culture according to a number of
dimensions, so that an observer might be able to make out its contours. Further
complicating the study, however, is the fact that no culture is completely
integrated. There will always be elements that contradict one another.
Additionally, culture evolves, so that at any given point in time, it contains
elements representing the past, the present, and the future. Moody-Adams
argued that the survival of any culture requires these apparent contradictions
as opportunities to doubt and question and ultimately adapt to changing circumstances (1997, pp. 70 f, 196, & 209).

One of the ways to study culture is hermeneutics, a process of interpretation. This method seeks the meaning behind the symbols, artifacts, and
practices that constitute a culture, so that people can understand one another.
Plainly, people within a culture have certain advantages in understanding one
another, inasmuch as they probably share a common language, experiences,
and what Gadamer called prejudices. Outsiders have more work to do. But
even within a culture, people must work to understand one another and get to
the meaning behind their various expressions. Since leadership depends on
shared understanding, it requires a degree of hermeneutics just to get the job
done right, let alone for an outsider to grasp what just happened. Leadership
scholars from outside of a given culture must work at understanding the data
that they gather.

The actual process by which a culture changes can rely on the unit of analysis
known as the generation, as explained by Ortega y Gasset. We saw that
a specific generation in England took on the perilous and uncertain project of
translating the Holy Bible into English, thereby changing the culture as a whole
for centuries to come. The details of that story exhibit very little leadership, in
the conventional sense of the term, and that is because it was such a shared
undertaking. Truly, the KJV was a collaboration. The example of Martin Luther
King, however, is quite different. Even though a generation of African
Americans and their allies took risks on behalf of the Civil Rights movement,
MLK became a symbol and thereby led the movement. Even then, we had to get
behind the personalities to the underlying source of friction that had confounded
the American experience all along, and that contradiction was the incompatibility of a Christian people operating a liberal democracy where racial codes
prevailed. At some point, the incongruity had to be addressed.

Leadership studies exists in part to appreciate the possibility and impact of agency within the prevailing context. The study of leadership entails an appreciation for the dynamics of culture, even if that story relies on a variety of useful fictions – among them, leadership itself. For leadership is as much a struggle over symbols as it is anything else. Culture is in this sense the field where leaders engage in these struggles.

Claude Lévi-Strauss (1956/1963) went to great lengths in his study of various cultures around the world to detect the dualities that structure communities. The cultures themselves usually differentiate men from women, children from adulthood, the sacred and the profane in an almost infinite number of ways, making distinctions that help to orient the members. To illustrate how this works, he wrote about dual organizations with at least two different types of bifurcation in the layout of villages. In one type, the village is split right down the middle in an almost mirror-like symmetry; these villages he referred to as *diametric structures*. In contemporary terms, we might picture places with rival high schools on either side of town. We even speak of kids growing up on "the other side of the tracks" – as though a line runs through a population that highlights a substantive difference. My children went to a high school that cultivated a real hatred of kids from the next town over. The feelings were mutual. In another type of bifurcation, however, the village is split between a center and a periphery; these villages he referred to as *concentric structures*. In contemporary terms, we speak of an inner city and the suburbs. With greater insight, therefore, Lévi-Strauss discovered that each "type" of village is integrated into a single layout, such that a village can have both a center (as opposed to a periphery) and a diameter. The two are not mutually exclusive. A village can be split east versus west and also inside versus outside. I happen to have grown up in such a town. Why do I mention this?

Obviously, a more complex structure can incorporate a host of other dualities, such as racial distinctions, socioeconomic distinctions, political affiliation, religious enclaves, and the like. But Lévi-Strauss, in his effort to keep the analysis simple, was interested in showing how the same village can be ordered according to multiple dichotomies if one were paying attention and knew what to look for. What interested Lévi-Strauss, given his recurring commitment to the model of differentiation and integration, was the presence of space and time for the sides to come together, as for example, at a temple or during a ritual dance. The interior divisions often have their purposes, but sometimes the residents unite and transcend their differences, as for example, for the common defense or at festivals. What this suggested to him is not a dual structure but a *tripartite* structure, not unlike a simple graphic of land and water on a horizontal plane, both underneath a common sky on the vertical plane. From within this more elaborate schema of a triangle, he was able to show the many ways that diverse peoples accomplished the same basic purposes that contribute to good order. These conceptual tools are thus available to us also, as we try to make sense of our complex society that often seems so hopelessly torn apart along so many different dimensions. One can always readily identify an A and a B, squabbling loudly and contributing to partisan rancor (see e.g. Sasse, 2018). Perhaps part of leadership includes being a partisan, a mediator, or one who transcends these divisions altogether.

It is no surprise that the place where the various "sides" come together is treated as sacred. Leaders emerge on behalf of the various sides in any community, but what is needed is also a kind of leadership that preserves and honors these sacred communal spaces, these integral moments, when warring oppositions kneel beneath a sheltering sky. It is for this type of leadership from a forthcoming generation that my Element was written.

At any given point in time, then, a culture will include both contradictions and compatibilities. Each of these has the potential to influence cultural dynamics, whether spurring a generation to resolve a contradiction (such as whether Christianity will tolerate race-based policies) or to increase and enhance the compatibilities (such as whether to conflate religion, politics, law, and economics under the rubric of Utilitarianism). Realistically, both contradictions and compatibilities are present, which means that each contributes to the dynamics a culture will undergo, as though tugging that culture in different directions.

We saw that Bill Buckley emerged from within a given culture (southern, capitalist/anticommunist, Catholic, conservative, and so forth), hoping to defend that culture as part of a larger project to uphold Western traditions, only to confront incompatibilities between his convictions and the race-based policies of Jim Crow. If anyone experienced the tug of these competing change mechanisms at the personal level, it was he. Leadership operates within this ongoing tension, trying to figure out when to persist and when to change – and perhaps more profoundly, trying to figure out what needs to persist and what needs to change.

Far be it from me to propose a simple and elegant formula for describing the engines of history. If anything, I have tried to emphasize that at any given point in time, culture itself is a mess, a vast and bewildering conglomeration of possibilities, populated by an array of sociological forms, comprised of elements from the past, the present, and the future – all pulling in different directions. Any purposeful shift requires collaborative behavior at the level of the generation – if not several generations – when a dedicated corps of committed change agents participate together in processes of leadership.

At all times, leadership inhabits culture, entrenching certain features of it as a patrimony, as Buckley set out to do as a young conservative firebrand, but also using other features in that culture to bring about wholesome change. Leaders are found to have access to an Archimedean point outside of that culture from which to judge, whether that vantage point originates in religion, law, philosophy, morality, or sensibilities, so that leadership, though it finds itself ineluctably immersed (if not entangled) in culture, also rises up in order to critique. And so they shape one another, culture and leadership, back and forth.

References

Alim, H. S., & Smitherman, G. (2012). *Articulate while Black: Barack Obama, Language, and Race in the US*. Oxford University Press.

Alter, R. (2010). *Pen of Iron: American Prose and the King James Bible*. Princeton University Press.

Alvesson, M. (1993). *Cultural Perspectives on Organizations*. Cambridge University Press.

Alvesson, M. (2002). *Understanding Organizational Culture*. Sage.

Alvesson, M. (2011). "Leadership and Organizational Culture." In Bryman, A., Collinson, D., Grint, K., Jackson, B., & Uhl-Bien, M. (eds.). *The Sage Handbook of Leadership* (pp. 151–164). Sage.

Archer, M. (1996). *Culture and Agency: The Place of Culture in Social Theory* (revised ed.). Cambridge University Press.

Baldwin, J., Faulkner, S., & Hecht, M. (2006). "A Moving Target: The Illusive Definition of Culture." In Baldwin, J., Faulkner, S., Hecht, M., & Lindsley, S. (eds.). *Redefining Culture: Perspectives across the Disciplines* (pp. 3–26). Lawrence Erlbaum Assoc.

Benedict, R. (1934/2005). *Patterns of Culture*. Mariner Books.

Benjamin, W. (1968). *Illuminations: Essays and Reflections* (H. Arendt, ed.). Mariner Books.

Bennett, J. (1974, April). "The Conscience of Huckleberry Finn." *Philosophy. 49*(188): 123–134.

Beran, M. (2021, July). "FDR's Tory Pragmatism." *National Review. 73*(13): 34–36.

Berlin, I. (1969/1979). "Vico's Concept of Knowledge." In Berlin, I (ed.). *Against the Current: Essays in the History of Ideas* (pp. 111–119). Penguin.

Berlin, I. (1978). *The Hedgehog and the Fox: An Essay on Tolstoy's View of History*. Phoenix.

Bernstein, R. (1997). "Pragmatism, Pluralism, and the Healing of Wounds." In L. Menand (ed.). *Pragmatism: A Reader* (pp. 382–401). Vintage Books.

Blass, T. (ed.). (1999). *Obedience to Authority: Current Perspectives on the Milgram Paradigm*. Psychology Press.

Bobrick, B. (2001). *Wide as the Waters: The Story of the English Bible and the Revolution It Inspired*. Penguin.

Bogus, C. (2011). *Buckley*. Bloomsbury Press.

Bradley, K., Cartledge, P., Drescher, S., et al. (eds.). (2011–2017). *The Cambridge World History of Slavery* (vols. 1–4). Cambridge University Press.

Bragg, M. (2011). *The Book of Books: The Radical Impact of the King James Bible 1611–2011*. Sceptre.

Brown, A. (2014). *The Myth of the Strong Leader*. Basic Books.

Brunner, E. (1949). *Christianity and Civilization* (part 2). Charles Scribner's Sons.

Bryman, A., Stephens, M., & Campo, C. (1996). "The Importance of Context: Qualitative Research and the Study of Leadership." *The Leadership Quarterly. 7*(3): 353–370.

Buccola, N. (2019). *The Fire Is upon Us: James Baldwin, William F. Buckley Jr., and the Debate over Race in America*. Princeton University Press.

Buckley, P., & Buckley, W. (eds.). (1979). *WFB: An Appreciation*. Privately printed.

Buckley, W. (1970). *The Governor Listeth: A Book of Inspired Political Revelations*. G. P. Putnam's Sons.

Buckley, W. (1989). *On the Firing Line: The Public Life of Our Public Figures*. Random House.

Buckley, W. (1997). *Nearer, My God*. Doubleday.

Buckley, W., & Kesler, C. (1988). *Keeping the Tablets: Modern American Conservative Thought*. HarperCollins.

The Cambridge Advanced Learner's Dictionary and Thesaurus. (2021). Cambridge University Press. Accessed on March 19, 2021 from https://dictionary.cambridge.org/dictionary/english/culture.

Campbell, G. (2010). *Bible: The Story of the King James Version 1611–2011*. Oxford University Press.

Carnap, R. (1934/1995). *The Unity of Science* (M. Black, trans.). Thoemmes Press.

Carroll, R., & Prickett, S. (2008). "Introduction." In Carroll, R., & Prickett, S. (eds.). *The Bible: Authorized King James Version*. Oxford University Press.

Cassirer, E. (1942/2000). *The Logic of the Cultural Sciences* (S. G. Lofts, trans.). Yale University Press.

Cassirer, E. (1946). *Language and Myth* (S. Langer, trans.). Dover.

Clough, M. (2002). "Cultural Anthropology." In Shriberg, A., Shriberg, D., & Lloyd, C. (eds.). *Practicing Leadership: Principles and Applications* (2nd ed.) (pp. 85–109). John Wiley & Sons.

Cohen, A. (2009, April). "Many Forms of Culture." *American Psychologist. 64* (3): 194–204.

Colvin, R. (1996). "Transformational Executive Leadership: A Comparison of Culture-Focused and Individual Focused Leadership Modalities." Dissertation, Virginia Commonwealth University.

Cooper, B. (2020). *Paleolithic Politics: The Human Community in Early Art.* University of Notre Dame Press.

Copi, I. (1978). *Introduction to Logic* (5th ed.). Macmillan Publishing Co.

de Landa, M. (2000). *A Thousand Years of Nonlinear History.* Swerve Books.

Den Hartog, D., & Dickson, M. (2004). "Leadership and Culture." In Antonakis, J., Cianciolo, A., & Sternberg, R. (eds.). *The Nature of Leadership* (pp. 249–278). Sage.

de Tarde, G. (1895/1903). *The Laws of Imitation* (E. C. Parsons, trans.). Henry Holt & Co.

Diggins, J. P. (1996). *Max Weber: Politics and the Spirit of Tragedy.* BasicBooks.

Donaldson, W. (2017). *Simple_Complexity: A Management Book for the Rest of Us.* Morgan James Publishing.

Dostal, R. (ed.). (2002). *The Cambridge Companion to Gadamer.* Cambridge University Press.

Dostoevsky, F. (1871–1872/2008). *Demons* (R. Maguire, trans.). Penguin Classics.

DuBois, W. E. B. (1995). "The Talented Tenth." Excerpted in T. Wren (ed.). *The Leader's Companion: Insights on Leadership through the Ages* (pp. 78–80). Free Press.

Durkheim, E. (1895/1938). *The Rules of Sociological Method* (S. Solovay & J. Mueller, trans.). Free Press.

Eagleton, T. (2000). *The Idea of Culture* [*Blackwell manifestos*]. Blackwell Publishing.

Fairholm, G. (1994). *Leadership and the Culture of Trust.* Praeger.

Faulkner, S., Baldwin, J., Lindsley, S., & Hecht, M. (2006). "Layers of Meaning: An Analysis of Definitions of Culture." In Baldwin, J., Faulkner, S., Hecht, M., & Lindsley, S. (eds.). *Redefining Culture: Perspectives across the Disciplines* (pp. 27–52). Lawrence Erlbaum Assoc.

Felzenberg, A. (2017, May 13). "How William F. Buckley, Jr., Changed His Mind on Civil Rights." *Politico.* Accessed on June 7, 2020 from www.politico.com /magazine/story/2017/05/13/william-f-buckley-civil-rights-215129.

Fiedler, F. E. (1972). "How Do You Make Leaders More Effective? New Answers to an Old Puzzle." *Organizational Dynamics. 1*(2): 3–18.

Fiske, D. (1986). "Specificity of Method and Knowledge in Social Science." In Fiske, D., & Schweder, R. (eds.) *Metatheory in Social Science: Pluralisms and Subjectivities* (pp. 61–82). University of Chicago Press.

Foucault, M. (1966/1994). *The Order of Things: An Archeology of the Human Sciences*. Vintage Books.

Freedman, A. (2021). *Thrive: The Leader's Guide to Building a High-Performance Culture*. Lioncrest Publishing.

Freud, S. (2005). *The Unconscious* (G. Frankland, trans.). Penguin Modern Classics.

Frye, R. (1965). "Introduction." In Frye, R. (ed.). *The Bible: Selections from the King James Version for Study as Literature* (pp. ix–xxxix). Houghton Mifflin.

Gadamer, H. G. (1976). *Philosophical Hermeneutics* (D. Linge, trans.). University of California Press.

Gallie, W. B. (1956). "Essentially Contested Concepts." *Proceedings of the Aristotelian Society*. 56: 167–198.

Gardner, H. (2006). *Changing Minds: The Art and Science of Changing Our Own and Other People's Minds* [*Leadership for the Common Good*]. Harvard Business Review Press.

Gardner, H., with Laskin, E. (1995). *Leading Minds: An Anatomy of Leadership*. Basic Books.

Gebhardt, J., & Cooper, B. (1995). "Editors' Introduction." In Voegelin, E. (ed.). *Collected Works* (vol. 1; pp. ix–xlii). Louisiana State University Press.

Geertz, C. (1973). *The Interpretation of Cultures: Selected Essays*. Basic Books.

Gelfand, M. (2019). *Rule Makers, Rule Breakers: Tight and Loose Cultures and the Secret Signals That Direct Our Lives*. Scribner.

Giddens, A. (1984). *The Constitution of Society: Outline of the Theory of Structuration*. University of California Press.

Giddens, A. (1993). *New Rules of Sociological Method* (2nd ed.). Stanford University Press.

Golding, W. (1954). *Lord of the Flies*. Faber and Faber.

Goldstein, L. (1957, Dec.). "On Defining Culture." *American Anthropologist*. 59(6): 1075–1081.

Graham, J. (1994). *A Pragmatist Philosophy of Life in Ortega y Gasset*. University of Missouri Press.

Gramsci, A. (2011). *Prison Notebooks* (A. Callari & J. Buttigieg, trans.). Columbia University Press.

Greenslade, S. L. (ed.). (1963). *The Cambridge History of the Bible*. Cambridge University Press.

Habermas, J. (1988). *On the Logic of the Social Sciences* (S. Weber Nicholson & J. Stark, trans.). MIT Press.

Harter, N. (2007). *Clearings in the Forest: On the Study of Leadership*. Purdue University Press.

Harter, N. (2015). *Leadership and Coherence: A Cognitive Approach.* Routledge.

Harter, N. (2017, October 18). "Martin Luther and the Translation of the Bible into German." *VoegelinView.* Accessed on October 11, 2021 from https://voegelinview.com/martin-luther-translation-bible-german/.

Harter, N. (2020). *Leadership across Boundaries: A Passage to Aporia.* Routledge.

Harvey, M., & Riggio, R. (eds.). (2012). *Leadership Studies: The Dialogue of Disciplines.* Edward Elgar.

Hatch, M. (1993, October). "The Dynamics of Organizational Culture." *Academy Management Review. 18*(4): 657–693.

Heath, H. F. (1991, May). "The Elizabethan Age." *Modern Language Quarterly. IV*(1): 1–5.

Hecht, M., Baldwin, J., & Faulkner, S. (2006). "The (In)conclusion of the Matter: Shifting Signs and Models of Culture." In Baldwin, J., Faulkner, S., Hecht, M., & Lindsley, S. (eds.). *Redefining Culture: Perspectives across the Disciplines* (pp. 53–73). Lawrence Erlbaum Assoc.

Heilke, T. (1990). *Voegelin on the Idea of Race: An Analysis of Modern European Racism.* Louisiana State University Press.

Helle, H. (2013). *Messages from Georg Simmel [Studies in Critical Social Sciences].* Haymarket Books.

Hendershot, H. (2016). *Open to Debate: How William F. Buckley Put Liberal America on the Firing Line.* Broadside Books.

Hillman, J. (1986/2016). "Bachelard's Lautréamont, or Psychoanalysis without a Patient." In E. Casey (ed.). *Uniform Edition of the Writings of James Hillman* (vol. 8; pp. 282–299). Spring Publications.

Hofstede, G. (1980). *Culture's Consequences: International Differences in Work-Related Values.* Sage.

Hofstede, G. (1993, Feb.). "Cultural Constraints in Management Theories." *Academy of Management Executive. 7*: 81–94, reprinted in Wren, T. (1995). *The Leader's Companion: Insights on Leadership through the Ages* (pp. 253–270). Free Press.

Hofstede, G., Hofstede, G. J., & Minkov, M. (2010). *Cultures and Organizations: Software of the Mind* (3rd ed.). McGraw-Hill.

House, R., Hanges, P., Javidan, M., Dorfman, P., & Gupta, V. (2004). *Culture, Leadership, and Organizations: The GLOBE Study of 62 Societies.* Sage.

Hummel, R. (2008). *The Bureaucratic Experience: The Post-modern Challenge* (5th ed.). Routledge.

Jahanbegloo, R. (1995). *Conversations with Isaiah Berlin.* Phoenix Press.

James, W. (1907). *Pragmatism: A New Name for Some Old Ways of Thinking.* Longmans, Green, and Co.

Johnson, S. (2001). *Emergence: The Connected Lives of Ants, Brains, Cities, and Software.* Scribner.

Judis, J. (1988). *William F. Buckley: Patron Saint of the Conservatives.* Simon & Schuster.

Jung, C. (1980). *Collected Works* (vol. 9; R. F. C. Hull, trans.). Princeton University Press.

Kantonen, T. A. (1972). *Man in the Eyes of God: Human Existence in the Light of the Lutheran Confessions.* CSS Publishing.

Kerr, S., & Jermier, J. M. (1978). "Substitutes for Leadership: Their Meaning and Measurement." *Organizational Behavior and Human Performance. 22* (3): 375–403.

Kolakowski, L. (1966/1972). *Positivist Philosophy: From Hume to the Vienna Circle* (N. Guterman, trans.). Penguin.

Kroeber, A. L., & Kluckhohn, C. (1963). *Culture: A Critical Review of Concepts and Definitions.* Vintage Books.

Kuhn, T. S. (2012). *The Structure of Scientific Revolutions* (50th anniversary ed.). University of Chicago Press.

Lachmann, R., Eshelman, R., & Davis, M. (1988). "Bakhtin and Carnival: Culture as Counter-culture." *Cultural Critique.* (11): 115–152.

Landy, M. (1986, spring). "Culture and Politics in the Work of Antonio Gramsci." *Boundary 2. 14*(3): 49–70.

Leavitt, H., & Lipman-Blumen, J. (1995, July–August). "Hot Groups." *Harvard Business Review.* Accessed on June 5, 2019 from https://hbr.org/1995/07/hot-groups.

Lévi-Strauss, C. (1956/1963). "Do Dual Organizations Exist?" In Lévi-Strauss, C. (ed.). *Structural Anthropology* (C. Jacobson & B. G. Schoepf, trans.) (pp. 132–166). Basic Books.

Lévi-Strauss, C. (1988/1991). *Conversations with Claude Lévi-Strauss* (P. Wissing, trans.). University of Chicago Press.

Levine, D. (1995). *Visions of the Sociological Tradition.* University of Chicago Press.

Lewin, K. (1944, Mar.). "A Research Approach to Leadership Problems." *Journal of Educational Sociology. 17*(7): 392–398.

Lewin, K. (1951). *Field Theory in Social Science: Selected Theoretical Papers.* Harper & Row.

Lincoln, A. (1953–1955). *The Collected Works* (R. Basler, ed.). Rutgers University Press.

Livermore, D. (2015). *Leading with Cultural Intelligence: The Real Secret to Success* (2nd ed.). AMACOM.

Lorenz, K. (1966). *On Aggression* (M. K. Wilson, trans.). Harcourt, Brace & World.

MacIntyre, A. (1997). *The Unconscious: A Conceptual Analysis*. Thoemmes Press.

Mahfouz, N. (1985/2000). *Akhenaten: Dweller in Truth* (T. Abu-Hassabo, trans.). Anchor.

Manz, C. C., & Sims Jr., H. P. (1991). "Superleadership: Beyond the Myth of Heroic Leadership." *Organizational Dynamics. 19*(4): 18–35.

McCusker, M., Foti, R., & Abraham, E. (2019). "Leadership Research Methods." In Riggio, R. (ed.) *What's Wrong with Leadership? Improving Leadership Research and Practice* (pp. 9–40). Routledge.

McGrath, A. (2001). *In the Beginning: The Story of the King James Bible and How It Changed a Nation, a Language, and a Culture*. Anchor Books.

McKeon, R. (1947). *Introduction to Aristotle*. Modern Library.

Meadows, D. H. (2008). *Thinking in Systems: A Primer*. Chelsea Green Publishing.

Meek, E. L. (2014). *A Little Manual for Knowing*. Cascade Books.

Menand, L. (2001). *The Metaphysical Club: A Story of Ideas in America*. Farrar, Straus, & Giroux.

Merton, R. (1976). *Sociological Ambivalence and Other Essays*. Free Press.

Moody-Adams, M. (1997). *Fieldwork in Familiar Places: Morality, Culture, & Philosophy*. Harvard University Press.

New York Times Magazine. (2019). "The 1619 Project." Accessed on June 5, 2020 from www.nytimes.com/interactive/2019/08/14/magazine/1619-america-slavery.html.

Nicolson, A. (2005). *God's Secretaries: The Making of the King James Bible*. Zondervan.

Niebuhr, H. R. (1951). *Christ and Culture*. Harper Torchlight.

Norton, D. (2011). *The King James Bible: A Short History from Tyndale to Today*. Cambridge University Press.

Oakes, G. (1980). "Introduction." In Simmel, G. (ed.). *Essays on Interpretation in Social Science* (G. Oakes, trans.). Rowman and Littlefield.

Oakes, K. (2021). *Culture Renovation: 18 Leadership Actions to Build an Unshakeable Company*. McGraw-Hill Education.

Ortegay Gasset, J. (1940/1946). *Concord and Liberty* (H. Weyl, trans.). W. W. Norton & Co.

Ortega y Gasset, J. (1932). *The Revolt of the Masses*. W. W. Norton & Co.

Ortega y Gasset, J. (1933/1961). *The Modern Theme* (J. Cleugh, trans.). W. W. Norton & Co.

Ortega y Gasset, J. (1957). *Man and People* (W. Trask, trans.). W. W. Norton & Co.

Ortega y Gasset, J. (1958). *Man and Crisis* (M. Adams, trans.). W. W. Norton & Co.

Osborn, R., Hunt, J., & Jauch, L. (2002, December). "Toward a Contextual Theory of Leadership." *Leadership Quarterly. 13*(6): 797–837.

Ospina, S., & Hittleman, M. (2011). "Thinking Sociologically about Leadership." In Harvey, M. & Riggio, R. (eds.). *Leadership Studies: The Dialogue of the Disciplines* (pp. 89–100). Edward Elgar.

Pareto, V. (1901/1991). *The Rise and Fall of Elites* (H. Zetterberg, trans.). Transaction.

Pelikan, J. (1985). *Jesus through the Centuries: His Place in the History of Culture.* Yale University Press.

Percy, W. (1954–1975). *The Message in the Bottle.* Picador.

Plutarch (2001). *Plutarch's Lives.* A. Hugh Clough (ed.). The Dryden translation. The Modern Library.

Polanyi, M. (2009). *The Tacit Dimension.* University of Chicago Press.

Quine, W. V., & Ullian, J. S. (1978). *The Web of Belief* (2nd ed.). McGraw-Hill.

Reuters. (2007, October 10). "President Misquoted over Gays in Iran: Aide." *Rueters.* Accessed on June 8, 2019 from www.reuters.com/article/us-iran-gays-idUSBLA05294620071010.

Rini, R. (2020). *The Ethics of Microaggression.* Routledge.

Roberts, K. A. (1978). "Toward a Generic Concept of Counter-culture." *Sociological Focus. 11*(2): 111–126.

Rosaldo, R. (2006). "Foreword." In Baldwin, J., Faulkner, S., Hecht, M., & Lindsley, S. (eds.). *Redefining Culture: Perspectives across the Disciplines* (pp. ix–xiii). Lawrence Erlbaum Assoc.

Ross, E. A. (1919). "Socialization." *American Journal of Sociology. 24*(6): 652–671.

Rost, J. (1993). *Leadership for the Twenty-first Century.* Praeger.

Rousseau, D. (1985). "Issues of Level in Organizational Research: Multi-level and Cross-level Perspectives." *Research in Organizational Behavior. 7*: 1–37.

Saintsbury, G. (1902). *A History of Elizabethan Literature.* Macmillan Company.

Sasse, B. (2018). *Them: Why We Hate Each Other – And How to Heal.* St. Martin's Press.

Schein, E. (1985) *Organizational Culture and Leadership* (1st ed.). Jossey-Bass.

Schein, E. (2004). *Organizational Culture and Leadership* (3rd ed.). Jossey-Bass.

Schmitt, C. (1976). *The Concept of the Political* (G. Schwab, trans.). Rutgers University Press.

Schouten, J., & McAlexander, J. (1995, June). "Subcultures of Consumption: An Ethnography of the New Bikers." *Journal of Consumer Research. 22*(1): 43–61.

Searle, J. (2006). "Social Ontology: Some Basic Principles." *Papers: Revista de sociologia. 80*: 51–71.

Simmel, G. (1908/1950). *The Sociology of Georg Simmel* (K. Wolff, trans.). Free Press.

Simmel, G. (1916/2005). *Rembrandt: An Essay in the Philosophy of Art* (A. Scott & H. Staubmann, trans.). Routledge.

Simmel, G. (1918/1997). "The Conflict of Modern Culture." In Simmel, G. (ed.). *Essays on Religion* (H. J. Helle & L. Nieder, trans.). Yale University Press.

Simmel, G. (1980). *Essays on Interpretation in Social Science* (G. Oakes, trans.). Rowman & Littlefield.

Simms, K. (2015). *Hans-Georg Gadamer (Routledge Critical Thinkers)*. Routledge.

Steinbock, A. (2003). "Generativity and the Scope of Generative Phenomenology." In D. Welton (ed.). *The New Husserl: A Critical Reader* (pp. 289–325). Indiana University Press.

Steinbock, A. J. (1998). "Husserl's Static and Genetic Phenomenology: Translator's Introduction to Two Essays. Essay 1: Static and Genetic Phenomenological Method. Essay 2: The Phenomenology of Monadic Individuality and the Phenomenology of the General Possibilities and Compossibilities of Lived-Experiences: Static and Genetic Phenomenology." *Continental Philosophy Review. 31*(2): 127–152.

Sugirtharajah, R. S. (2011). "Postcolonial Notes on the KJB." In Hamlin, H., & Jones, N. (eds.). *The King James Bible after 400 Years: Literary, Linguistic, and Cultural Influences*. Cambridge University Press.

Taylor, P. J. (1999). *Modernities: A Geohistorical Interpretation*. University of Minnesota Press.

Trice, H., & Beyer, J. (1991, May). "Cultural Leadership in Organizations." *Organization Science. 2*(2): 149–169.

Twain, M. (1885). *The Adventures of Huckleberry Finn: Tom Sawyer's Comrade*. Charles L. Webster & Co.

Tylor, E. B. (1871). *Primitive Culture: Researches into the Development of Mythology, Philosophy, Religion, Art, and Custom* (vol. 2). Murray.

van Cleve, D. (2021). *The Clarity Effect: Simple Leadership Principles to Create a Culture of Purpose, Passion, and Performance*. CRC Publishing.

Voegelin, E. (1956). *Order & History* (vol. 1). Louisiana State University Press.

Voegelin, E. (2007). *Collected Works* (vol. 30). University of Missouri Press.

Wang, X., Chen, Z., Shi, B., & Chen, H. (2021). "Tight Cultures Breed Dehumanization: An Interdisciplinary Approach. Accessed on August 5, 2021 from https://assets.researchsquare.com/files/rs-604817/v1/bf563095-ff85-4452-ad3e-c1da8ba1b355.pdf?c=1624387932.

Weber, M. (1958). *The Protestant Ethic and the Spirit of Capitalism* (T. Parsons, trans.). Scribner.

Whitehead, A. N. (1927). *Symbolism: Its Meaning and Effect*. Capricorn Books.

Wilber, K. (1998). *The Marriage of Sense and Soul*. Broadway Books.

Williams, H. (1894). "Kant's Doctrine of the Schemata." *The Monist. 4*(3): 375–384. Accessed on June 26, 2016 from www.jstor.org/stable/27897156.

Wilson, S. (2016). *Thinking Differently about Leadership: A Critical History of Leadership Studies*. Edward Elgar.

Wittgenstein, L. (1980). *Culture and Value* (P. Winch, trans.). University of Chicago Press.

Wren, J. T., & Swatez, M. J. (1995). "The Historical and Contemporary Contexts of Leadership: A Conceptual Model." In T. Wren (ed.). *The Leader's Companion: Insights on Leadership through the Ages* (pp. 245–252). The Free Press.

Yammarino, F., & Dionne, S. (2019). "Leadership and Levels of Analysis." In Riggio, R. (ed.) *What's Wrong with Leadership? Improving Leadership Research and Practice* (ch. 2 pp. 41–57). Routledge.

Yammarino, F., & Gooty, J. (2017). "Multi-level Issues and Dyads in Leadership Research." In Schyns, B., Hall, R., & Neves, P. (eds.). *Handbook of Methods in Leadership Research* (pp. 229–255). Edward Elgar.

Yukl, G. (2013). *Leadership in Organizations* (8th ed.). Pearson.

Acknowledgments

I want to say thank you publicly to Sarah Chace, Bob Colvin, Brent Cusher, William Donaldson, Michael Harvey, Joan McMahon, Jonathan Reams, Ron Riggio, Angela Spranger, and Qingyan Tian. For some time, I have shared these topics with my private study group at Christopher Newport University in Newport News, Virginia, a gathering of selected undergraduates whose practice of dialogue is the professional highlight of my week. More concretely, in the spring of 2021, I was permitted to introduce an undergraduate course that relied on many of these lessons, so to my colleague Kat Callahan and to those intrepid students in LDSP 464 Leadership in Complex Contexts, I offer my thanks. The many professionals at Cambridge University Press, whom I admire, have shepherded this project through to completion, with special thanks to Valerie Appleby, Shalini Bisa, Toby Ginsberg, Mathivathini Mareesan, Abigail Neale, and Annie Toynbee, in addition to their generous reviewers. Furthermore, the series editors have done a commendable job from start to finish.

This work was supported in part by a sabbatical leave from Christopher Newport University, Newport News, Virginia.

To God be all the glory. And to Karin, until my dying day, this heart.

This project is dedicated to my undergraduate students since August 1989 who keep me honest and keep me young, and who will shape the culture together

Cambridge Elements ≡

Leadership

Ronald Riggio
Claremont McKenna College

Ronald E. Riggio, Ph.D. is the Henry R. Kravis Professor of Leadership and Organisational Psychology and former Director of the Kravis Leadership Institute at Claremont McKenna College. Dr. Riggio is a psychologist and leadership scholar with over a dozen authored or edited books and more than 150 articles/book chapters. He has worked as a consultant, and serves on multiple editorial boards.

Susan Murphy
University of Edinburgh

Susan E. Murphy is Chair in Leadership Development at the University of Edinburgh Business School. She has published numerous articles and book chapters on leadership, leadership development, and mentoring. Susan was formerly Director of the School of Strategic Leadership Studies at James Madison University and Professor of Leadership Studies. Prior to that, she served as faculty and associate director of the Henry R. Kravis Leadership Institute at Claremont McKenna College. She also serves on the editorial board of The Leadership Quarterly.

Georgia Sorenson
University of Cambridge

The late Georgia Sorenson, Ph.D. was the James MacGregor Burns Leadership Scholar at the Moller Institute and Moller By-Fellow of Churchill College at Cambridge University. Before coming to Cambridge, she founded the James MacGregor Burns Academy of Leadership at the University of Maryland, where she was Distinguished Research Professor. An architect of the leadership studies field, Dr. Sorenson has authored numerous books and refereed journal articles.

Micha Popper, *University of Haifa*
Terry Price, *University of Richmond*
Krish Raval, *University of Oxford*
Roni Reiter-Palmon, *University of Nebraska*
Birgit Schyns, *Durham University*
Gillian Secrett, *University of Cambridge*
Nicholas Warner, *Claremont McKenna College*

About the series

Cambridge Elements in Leadership is multi- and inter-disciplinary, and will have broad appeal for leadership courses in Schools of Business, Education, Engineering, Public Policy, and in the Social Sciences and Humanities

Cambridge Elements ≡

Leadership

Elements in the series

Leadership Studies and the Desire for Shared Agreement
Stan Amaladas

Leading the Future of Technology
Rebecca LaForgia

Cultural Dynamics and Leadership
Nathan W. Harter

A full series listing is available at: www.cambridge.org/CELE

Made in the USA
Monee, IL
06 January 2023

24703391R00050